David N. Skinner

The Countryside of the

ANTONINE WALL

A Survey and Recommended Policy Statement

Published by the Countryside Commission for Scotland, Perth.   © 1973

ISBN 0 902226 20 7   Price £5

contents

Printed in Scotland by WOODS OF PERTH (Printers) LTD., 3/5 Mill Street, Perth

FOREWORD

The countryside of the Antonine Wall presents a range of complex problems of conservation and protection. It is not simply a series of historic sites, nor just a line across the Central Lowlands of Scotland, but a belt which has no easily defined natural boundaries, and which crosses several administrative areas. It is no easy task to identify policies and priorities in such an area. In this report, prepared for the Countryside Commission for Scotland, David Skinner puts forward strategies which are the result of detailed investigation and should be studied by all those responsible for the conservation of the wall.

The report goes beyond a plea for the protection of sections of the wall and looks at the nature of the countryside in which the whole length of wall lies, and at the larger issues which affect countryside planning in the Central Belt of Scotland. By looking at the countryside of the wall in its entirety, and by using new techniques of analysis and presentation, David Skinner has produced a report which we would recommend not only to those with a direct involvement in the conservation of the wall, but to planners and landscape architects throughout Scotland and beyond.

Until Mr Skinner's report has been thoroughly studied, it cannot of course commit anyone, including the Commission. Nevertheless we do urge that it be debated widely and that all appropriate bodies, in both public and private sectors, identify those areas in which they might contribute towards the solutions suggested by Mr Skinner and give earnest thought to how best they can help to achieve his deeply considered aims. There could be no better way of ensuring that this important national asset is not further diminished or impaired.

John Foster FRICS, FRTPI, ARIBA
Director, Countryside Commission
for Scotland

December 1973.

introduction

* Throughout this study small dimensions are given in metric quantities, but the mile, a Roman invention, is retained for larger ones, and the spacing of Forts may be read in miles directly from Figure 2.

The Antonine Wall was built in the second century A.D. to form the most north-westerly frontier of the Roman Empire. It is 37 miles* long and runs from the Firth of Forth to the Firth of Clyde, marking off the northern barbarians from the Empire.

Little of the Rampart of the Wall, which was built of turf, remains today, but substantial lengths of the great Ditch, which was dug in front of the Rampart, remain to be seen, and a good deal of the archaeology of the Wall and its associated Forts and Camps remains below ground. Unfortunately the Wall no longer lies through open country but passes through the modern settlements of Bo'ness, Laurieston, Falkirk, Bonnybridge, Twechar, Kirkintilloch, Bearsden and Clydebank to Old Kilpatrick.

Anticipating mounting threats to the environment of the Wall, the Countryside Commission for Scotland instructed me to make this study of its present appearance and use; to make a policy statement about its future conservation, and to recommend the main opportunities for the implementation of the proposed policy. The objective of conserving the environment of the Wall was assumed as part of the brief and the study was not required to justify this objective.

The autumn of 1972 was spent in getting to know the terrain and in collecting background information from the many agencies with interests in the Countryside of the Wall, and the text was written in the spring of 1973.

Most readers of this study are unlikely to have a clear idea of the location of the Wall, because no modern transport lines, which allow it to be visualised, follow it except for short lengths. The map in the back pocket will give the quickest reference for orienting those readers not already familiar with the Wall line. The names of Forts will also be strange to most readers, and these, together with the names of modern towns, will be found shown clearly on Figure 1b. Where names are used which are not to be found in Figure 1b the location of the place is described in a footnote to its first use, or a place may be located by its mileage measured from the east end of the Wall where no suitable place name exists.

David N. Skinner, A.R.I.B.A., A.I.L.A.
1 Argyle Place, Edinburgh EH9 1JU.

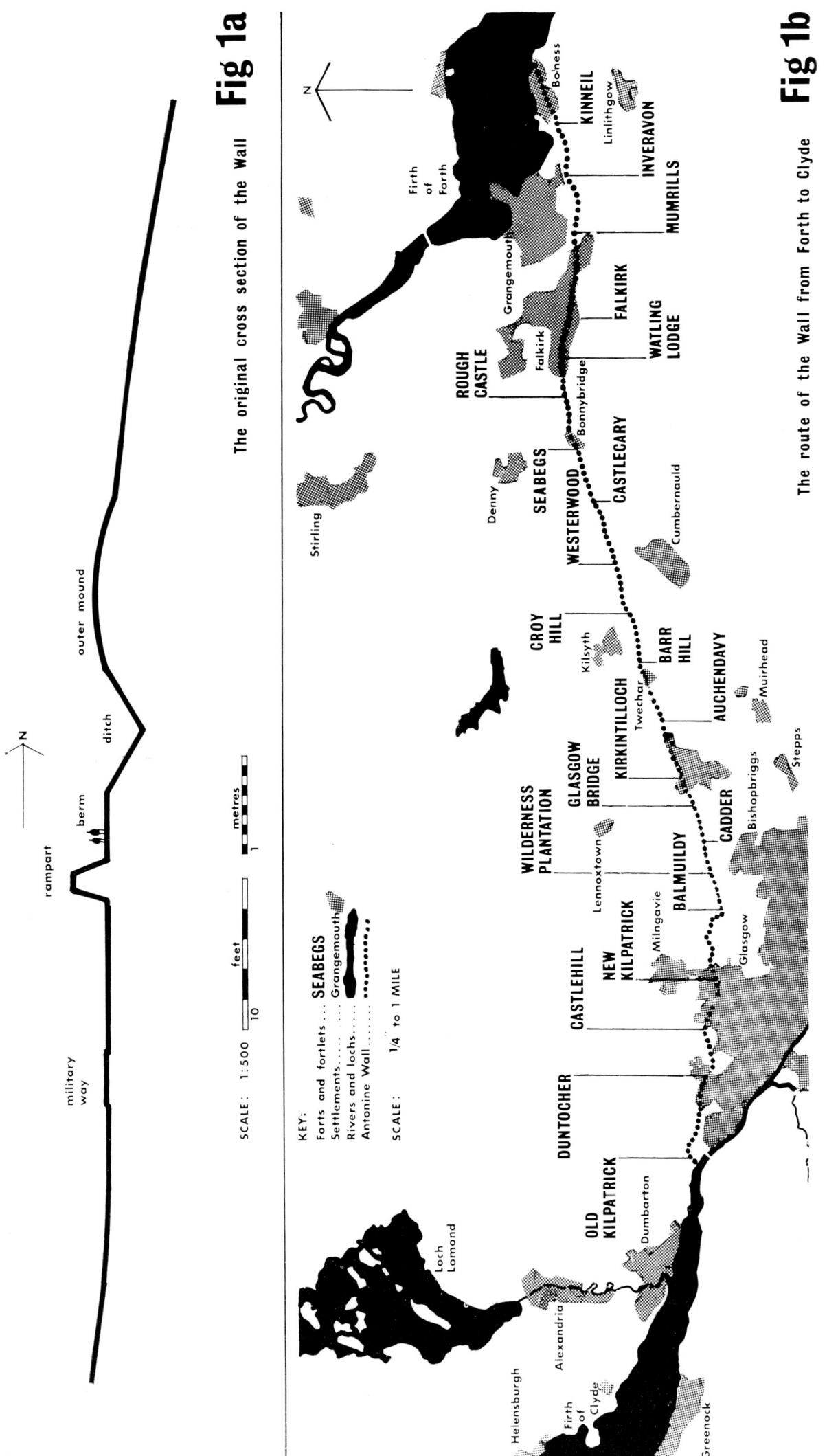

Fig 1a

The original cross section of the Wall

SCALE: 1:500

Fig 1b

The route of the Wall from Forth to Clyde

KEY:

Forts and fortlets.... **SEABEGS**

Settlements.......... Grangemouth

Rivers and lochs......

Antonine Wall........

SCALE: 1/4" to 1 MILE

1 the historical and archaeological Background

This study of the Antonine Wall is concerned principally with modern-day problems of Planning, Conservation and Recreation, and very little with history and archaeology, but it is impossible to discuss adequately the problems of the present day without at least an outline description of the main components of the Roman occupation and frontier works along the Wall line.

Sources of Information

Published material on the Wall is very extensive, as there has been a long series of excavations there dating from 1890 to the present day which have yielded a wealth of material. The description given below is based on the invaluable handbook prepared as a field guide to the Wall by Dr. Anne S. Robertson, entitled *The Antonine Wall* (published by the Glasgow Archaeological Society) and on information gained in conversation with her and with members of the staff of the Department of the Environment.

Setting Within the Roman Empire

The Romans constructed frontier works not only at the sites of Hadrian's and Antonine's Walls, but also across northern Europe, in Asia Minor, in Syria and in North Africa, in many of which places nothing now remains to be seen. Hadrian's Wall is the finest survivor of these great linear barriers, both on account of its excellent preservation and of its fine topographic setting. It is so obviously superior to the Antonine Wall in these respects that the importance of the latter has not been so clearly imprinted on the public consciousness. Although not so fine as Hadrian's Wall, the well-preserved sections of the Antonine Wall compare very favourably with those parts of the Roman Frontier which remain in Germany and in North Africa, which comprise the principal frontier remains outside Britain.

Interconnections with Hadrian's Wall

The frontier works are all different, each having its own characteristics, and were constructed at various times between about A.D. 80 and 160, and modified right up to the end of the Empire in the light of changing political and military conditions. The Antonine Wall, one of the latest frontier barriers to be built, contains modifications learned from building and operating Hadrian's Wall, while Hadrian's Wall itself was later modified as a result of experience gained on the Antonine Wall. The Antonine Wall is, therefore, not an isolated phenomenon but part of the political and military history not only of the province of Roman Britain but of the Roman Empire as a whole.

It is clear that Hadrian's Wall, Antonine's Wall and the complex of Roman roads and associated Forts which runs between and beyond them provide a remarkable opportunity for the study and demonstration of the Roman expansion and colonising process, and one which at least in respect of the physical military remains cannot be paralleled in any other part of their far-flung Empire.

Siting of the Wall

The Wall was not so much intended as a defensive position to be defended in the manner of a fortress under seige, but as an instrument for keeping an administrative control over the movements of natives, warlike and otherwise, for defining the limits of the Empire and to form at the same time the basis for military deployment and operations. No doubt it was also intended to overawe the Northern Britons with its proof of the capabilities of Roman might and technology. Nevertheless, it was laid out with a keen eye for topography, the defensive advantages of the ground being exploited wherever possible.

As the threat was principally from the north, the most desirable siting was on or above a north-facing slope with a wide field of view. With only a few gaps it was possible to site the Wall on a north-facing slope for the first* 28½ miles as far as Balmuildy Fort, but beyond this mixed terrain begins, with increasingly difficult ground for finding defensive positions, while in the last few miles to Old Kilpatrick the Wall lies on a south-facing slope, menaced from the steep Kilpatrick Braes to the north.

The Construction of the Wall

The Antonine Frontier as conjectured today consists of a complex including the Wall, Forts, Camps, Fortlets†, Roads, possible Signalling Stations and possible Civil Settlements. The numbers, dispositions and uses of all these features are not entirely agreed, but a

great deal is known about them, and in particular the Wall itself has been well investigated.

The Forts etc. vary greatly in size and to some extent in construction, but the linear frontier barrier shows every sign of having been constructed to a uniform specification with only occasional variations.

The Rampart was built of turf on a stone foundation, the width of which has suggested a wall of about 3 metres in height with a 2 metre wide top. Above this a wooden walkway with a protective wooden wall on the northern side are presumed, bringing the total height to around 5 metres. On the north side of the Rampart a Ditch was dug about 3.5 metres deep and averaging 12 metres wide with a V section. The distance between the base of the Rampart and the edge of the Ditch varies, but there is generally a shelf at least 7 metres wide, and sometimes much more. The material dug from the Ditch was thrown out on the north side, where it was either scattered or built into an outer mound. The general scheme may be pictured from the scale section Figure 1a.

Behind the Wall, and more or less parallel with it at a distance of about 80-90 metres to the south, ran a road now known as the Military Way; this connected the Forts and provided a safe, guarded communication route. While the location of the Wall is known with only a few uncertainties throughout its length, the line of the Military Way has only been established at a few places, and is now visible in only one location at Seabegs Wood, near Bonnybridge.

The frontier works are thought to have been manned from Forts at two mile intervals along the Wall, and thirteen Fort sites have been identified, leaving proof of six missing Forts still to be established in detail, although the Ordnance Survey map of the Antonine Wall shows all nineteen Forts on the assumption that the two mile spacing is correct.

Unlike the Wall, there is no standard Fort specification, neither for the initial construction nor for the amendments to their arrangements which were required during the course of their occupancy, which lasted for about two generations.

*The Wall is built from East to West, and it is convenient to consider it in that sense in describing it.

† The distinction between Forts and Fortlets made by Dr. Robertson is followed as distinct from that made by the Ordnance Survey.

5

* Evidence from aerial photography gives knowledge of at least the main lines of the other three, which are Carriden, Auchendavy and Castlehill. Excavated Forts are Mumrills, Rough Castle, Castlecary, Westerwood, Croy Hill, Bar Hill, Cadder, Balmuildy, Duntocher and Old Kilpatrick. Yet to be accurately located are Kinneil, Inveravon, Falkirk, Seabegs, Kirkintilloch (New Kilpatrick) at least three of which are built over.

Ten of the thirteen known Forts have been excavated* and of those unexcavated Castlehill Fort has been deliberately set aside in the expectation that more advanced excavation methods may yet be found, thus giving later archaeologists an undisturbed Roman site to work on.

The outer walls of Forts were of turf except in two cases, Castlecary and Balmuildy, where they were constructed in stone. As turf construction is particularly liable to destruction when left exposed to the weather, the excavations which have revealed these features have had to be filled in again in order to protect them, after whatever knowledge they have yielded has been recorded.

The stone constructions have not survived the years any better than the turf. They no doubt formed a useful quarry for cut stone to later generations of builders. The existence of stone walls at Castlecary and Balmuildy has some importance from the point of view of display of the Forts today, because an authentic restoration of these walls, or the bases of them, could be made in stone and this could allow them to remain exposed.

The Camps which have been discovered so far are somewhat detached from the Wall as a rule, and are little more than faint rectangles on the ground. Little needs to be said about them here, but their existence is taken into account in the later sections dealing with planning matters.

Some of the most interesting finds in connection with the Frontier have been from Civil Settlements associated with the Forts. No Civil Settlement has been fully excavated and its form recorded, but their existence is known or suspected close to the majority of Forts.

The Prospects for Further Archaeological Discovery

The route and form of the Rampart and Ditch being known, and over half the Forts having been excavated, the field of possible future discovery along the Frontier has been sharply narrowed.

In respect of the Rampart and Ditch the most which may be expected from further excavation is greater precision as to its exact position in sections where it is invisible, more extensive information about such technical details as the handling of drainage through culverts, or possible reasons why the foundation width was altered by small amounts.

However, it is only recently that the sites of some of the Forts and Camps have been revealed by aerial photographs, and it is impossible to anticipate what further technical advance may make possible. There is still controversy about the purposes of certain Fortlets and the existence of others, and the use of the supposed Signalling Stations (platforms for lighting beacon fires) is still under discussion.

The Civil Settlements could still yield much illuminating new material, as none of them has yet been systematically investigated.

Energy expended on the Frontier so far by archaeologists has been aimed at preserving the sites and extracting information from them. The work of displaying and explaining the nature of the Roman military presence at this most remote corner of the Empire to the public has hardly been begun, and it may be that this is where the greatest challenge lies in the immediate future.

AIR PHOTO 1: ROUGH CASTLE FROM THE EAST
The Ditch of the Wall runs from the bottom to the top of the picture, and the
Fort lies on the left of the Ditch and shows as a series of more or less
rectangular outlines. The pits called 'lilia' can be clearly seen on the right of
the Ditch almost surrounded by woodland. Some of the many overhead
electricity lines which mar this area can be seen crossing the picture from
north to south.

2 the appearance of the wall today

The Land Use Pattern and the Wall

In A.D. 160 the Antonine Frontier was the mightiest work of man north of Hadrian's Wall, producing a new order and polarity which must have astonished the natives. The logic of this Roman Order was wholly military. When military ordering of the land gave way to more peaceful development in later centuries a new logic led to a network of routes and settlements which, although utilising lengths of the Wall here and there, basically ignored it.

In the 19th century the logic of engineering led to a choice of routes which paralleled the general line of the Wall for 20 miles in the case of the Forth and Clyde Canal,* and 9 miles in the case of the railway, but in spite of this support the clarity of the Roman idea is blurred in the mind by our inability to travel along the whole Wall line by any modern route, or even to find it without the aid of some map reading ability.

Following the Wall today calls for stout shoes and a course set across country. The walker must cross fields both arable and grazing, woods, golf courses and parks; he must pass through sand quarries and over shale tips, and he must circumvent private gardens, factories and towns. The canal crosses the Wall four times, and railway lines eight times not counting crossings in built-up areas. It is cut by the River Avon and the River Kelvin, and by roads too numerous to mention, including the M9 at Polmont, the A80 at Castlecary and the A82 at Old Kilpatrick, to name only those with dual carriageways.

The Identification of the Wall in the Landscape

In spite of this fragmentation there are at intervals throughout its length features which allow its line to be identified from a distance by the observer who knows what to look for (even though he may not readily be able to follow the route except across country). The siting of the Wall on the north-facing slope for the first 28½ miles has already been mentioned. From time to time this north-facing slope steepens into an escarpment, as between Bo'ness and Polmont, between Castlecary and Dullatur, at Croy Hill and at Bar Hill, and when it does so the line of the Wall can be clearly

References to the canal below always intend the Forth and Clyde Canal; the Union Canal is not part of the Countryside of the Wall.

8

imagined. In the last $8\frac{1}{2}$ miles where north-facing slopes were not available, the three small hills of Crow Hill*, Castlehill and Duntocher stand up prominently on the Wall line. The latter two had a Fort on their summits. In particular, Castlehill is distinguished by a ring of trees around the Fort, which gives it an added impact.

In a number of other places the line of the Wall is distinguishable due to lines of trees, hedgerows or woodland edges which give the eye a line to follow when seen from a distance. Nowhere is the actual Rampart or Ditch visible from any position off the line of the Wall, although occasionally the Ditch may be seen some distance ahead by a person already on its line.

Viewpoints

The most notable viewpoints from which the line of the Wall may be followed for some distance are from Beancross† looking along the escarpment to the east, from Croy Hill, Bar Hill, Crow Hill, Castlehill and Duntocher, all looking both east and west. The longest view is from Beancross, being three to four miles of the escarpment landscape. Crow Hill affords an eastward view of about two miles, and the others are correspondingly less.

Actual Remains, as Distinct from the Wall Line

The location of the Wall in the landscape by identifying escarpments, tree lines or other guides is a different issue from that of finding the actual form of the remains on the ground.

Remains of Forts

Easily visible remains of Forts are few, but it so happens that the best of them at Rough Castle are not only visible from the line of the Wall itself, but may also be glimpsed from the main Edinburgh-Glasgow railway line. The view is of a series of low mounds forming ramparts to the Fort about one metre high. In theory the Fort at Castlecary might also be visible from the train, but in practice the speed with which it goes right through the middle of the Fort, and the faintness of the remains, makes this impossible. Other Forts may show traces on the ground which may be searched out by enthusiasts, but nothing impressive remains above ground.

Remains of the Wall

The impressive remains of the Wall are principally its Ditch component, except in two favoured locations, Rough Castle and Seabegs, where the base of a Rampart up to $1\frac{1}{2}$ metres high can be seen for a total of about two miles. There are other stretches where traces of the Rampart may still be seen in less favourable circumstances, at lesser heights and over short distances.

Where the Ditch is well defined, as at Watling Lodge, Rough Castle and Croy Hill, it is most impressive, particularly at Croy Hill where it surmounts a steep incline and makes an angle which shows it to particular advantage.

More often, however, the Ditch is represented by a hollow of much smaller dimensions than the original, and the size of this hollow may be anything from a fairly well marked trench to the faintest undulation. Very often it takes a keen eye to detect a dip at all, and for long distances no trace of the Wall remains.

A division of the Wall into five grades is helpful in describing it for the purposes of this study; the grades are intended only as a guide to appearance, and have no archaeological significance.

Grade 1. In this grade the Ditch is at something approaching its original dimensions, or if somewhat filled in, is accompanied by remains of the Rampart, which increases its importance.

1a. Ditch full-size, Rampart visible. This only occurs at Rough Castle.

1b. Ditch nearly full size, Rampart visible. This only occurs in Seabegs Wood.

1c. Ditch full size, no Rampart. This only occurs at Watling Lodge and Dullatur.

Grade 2. Ditch well defined but not full size.

2a. Ditch well defined and highly impressive. This occurs on Croy Hill, where the rough grass on an open hillside gives it greater impact than the same sized ditch in less favourable circumstances.

2b. Ditch well defined but not particularly impressive. This occurs more frequently than the descriptions above. Examples would be found near Westerwood and

Crow Hill lies midway between Balmuildy and Bearsden.

†Beancross lies on the Wall about 1 mile east of Mumrills.

9

PLATE ONE: The Wall at Rough Castle   Grade 1a

Callendar Park is at the east end of Falkirk.

in Callendar Park*, where the steep V section of the Ditch has been rounded out, but it is still at least 2 metres deep.

Grade 3. Ditch indistinct or nominal. This would describe a situation where the trench has been so rounded out that it might be mistaken for a natural minor undulation of the land. An example might be the stretch of Wall east of Castlecary.

Grade 4. Rampart Foundation exposed for public inspection. This occurs at two places in Bearsden, and one in Duntocher.

Grade 5. No trace of Wall now visible.

This classification does not do justice to those sections of the Wall where there are some remains of Rampart next to Ditch of well-defined or lesser status, but these are very short sections and their non-recognition is not likely to affect the later conclusions.

Plates 1-6 show examples of these various conditions of preservation.

Plate 1. The best preserved part of the Wal at Rough Castle, showing sharply cut Ditch and remains of Rampart. Grade 1a. (Page 10)

Plate 2. An excellently preserved section of Ditch only, at Watling Lodge. Grade 1c. (Page 11)

Plate 3. Well-defined Ditch at Callendar Park. Grade 2b. (Page 13)

Plate 4. Nominal Ditch at Castlecary School. Grade 3. (Page 14)

Plate 5. Exposed Foundation of the Rampart in a cemetery in Bearsden. Grade 4. (Page 15)

Plate 6. The line of the Wall descending to the Clyde, with no visible trace. (Page 18)

Plates 1-6 illustrate a graded series of views of the Wall which can be referred to in connection with Figure 2, which is now to be described. Other views of the Wall can be seen in Plates 9 and 10, and in particular the sections already mentioned at Croy Hill and Seabegs Wood may be seen at Plate 9, and a further view of Rough Castle at Plate 10.

Photographic Coverage of the Wall

It would be desirable to include here a good photographic survey of the Wall, so that its character could be understood by the reader in some detail, but the complexity of its circumstances makes it impossible to include more than a small selection of the possible illustrations. Instead, those elements which are amenable to statistical presentation or presentation by graph are followed through in the next Chapter, and Chapter 8 gives a description based on the thirty-six photographs reproduced in Plates 9 and 10. The reason for including these Plates at the end of the study rather than at the beginning is so that the accompanying text may appropriately introduce some of the planning and design points which are dealt with in Chapters 4 to 7, as well as the purely descriptive material of Chapters 2 and 3.

The three air photographs (pages 7, 35 and 61) show some of the best preserved lengths of Wall, but at the same time illustrate many of the diverse problems dealt with in chapters 2 to 7.

PLATE FOUR: Nominal Ditch at Castlecary School   Grade 3

3 chart presentation of wall data

Already in Chapter 2 parts of the Wall have been indicated as more easily identifiable in the landscape than others, the variety of land uses through which the Wall passes has already been touched on, and should now be related to the factors of appearance, and quite a complicated pattern begins to emerge. As the subjects of ease of movement and ease of access along the Wall are added to the picture, the inter-relationships become too complicated to handle except in a very cumbersome text. For this reason a chart (Figure 2, facing) has been devised with the object of allowing a ready assessment to be made of those factors which occur together in any length of the Wall.

This chart is laid out to a 37 mile (M) long scale representing the total Wall length, and the subdivision of this scale permits the recording of uses and character to limits of one-twentieth of a mile.

Chart Information

Lines 3-6	The four grades of appearance of the Wall remains which have been described in Chapter 2.
Line 7	The sections with steep escarpment and identifying tree lines etc. as already described in Chapter 2.
Lines 8-9	The sections with good views along the Wall, allowing an appreciation of its route.
Lines 10-19	The character of the land immediately beside the Wall.
Lines 20-29	The character of the more distant views.
Lines 30-34	The ease of getting along the Wall on foot due to the nature of the terrain.
Lines 35-41	The ease of getting access along the Wall due to barriers of private ownership, motorways etc.
Lines 50-66	The land uses along the Wall.

Other information on the chart is referred to in later chapters.

All the columns are summarised as percentages of the total length of the Wall, which should allow an accurate grasp to be made of the basic factors relating to it.

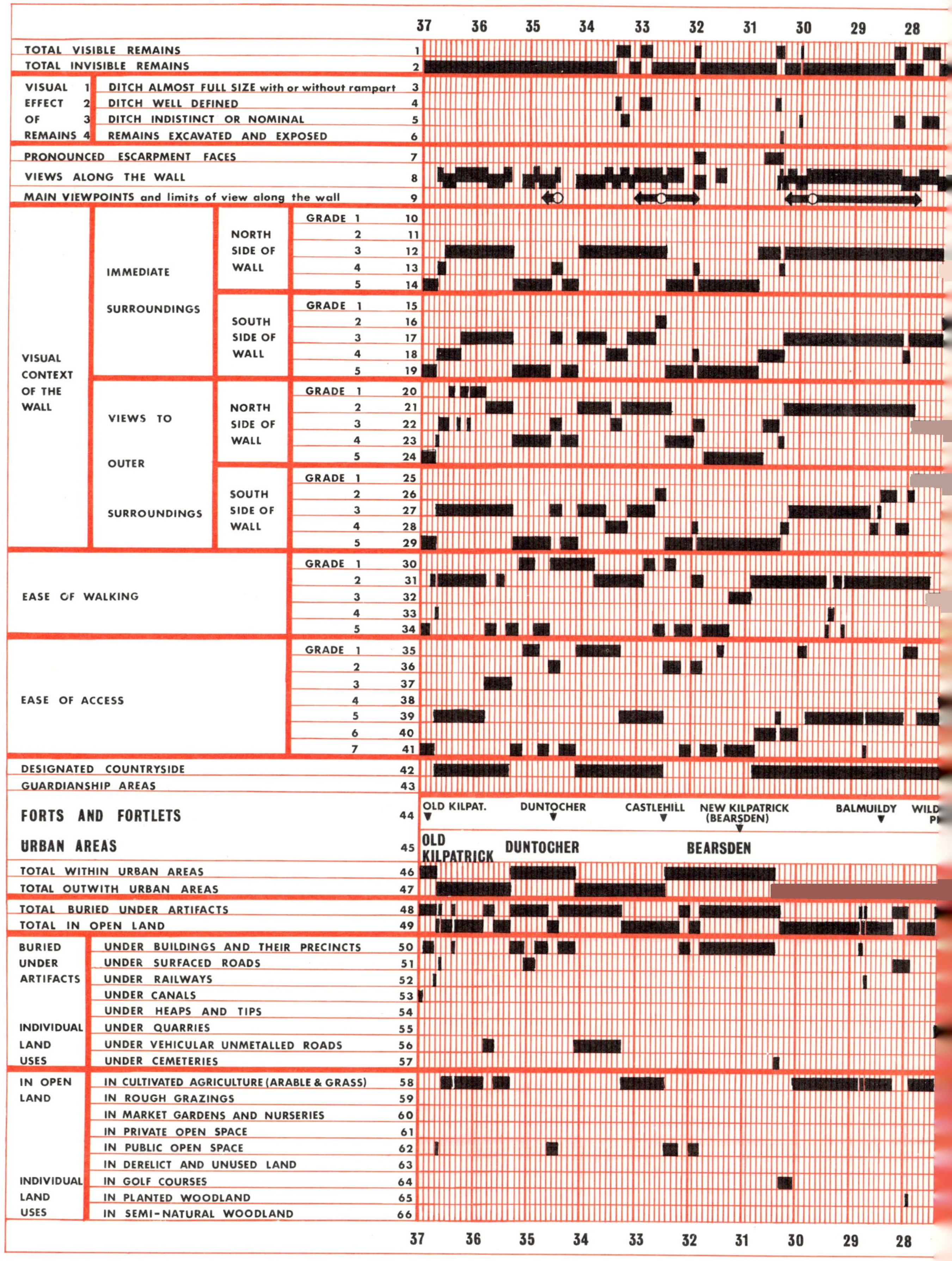

37 36 35 34 33 32 31 30 29 28
TOTAL VISIBLE REMAINS 1
TOTAL INVISIBLE REMAINS 2
VISUAL EFFECT OF REMAINS
1 DITCH ALMOST FULL SIZE with or without rampart 3
2 DITCH WELL DEFINED 4
3 DITCH INDISTINCT OR NOMINAL 5
4 REMAINS EXCAVATED AND EXPOSED 6
PRONOUNCED ESCARPMENT FACES 7
VIEWS ALONG THE WALL 8
MAIN VIEWPOINTS and limits of view along the wall 9
VISUAL CONTEXT OF THE WALL
IMMEDIATE SURROUNDINGS
NORTH SIDE OF WALL
GRADE 1 10
2 11
3 12
4 13
5 14
SOUTH SIDE OF WALL
GRADE 1 15
2 16
3 17
4 18
5 19
VIEWS TO OUTER SURROUNDINGS
NORTH SIDE OF WALL
GRADE 1 20
2 21
3 22
4 23
5 24
SOUTH SIDE OF WALL
GRADE 1 25
2 26
3 27
4 28
5 29
EASE OF WALKING
GRADE 1 30
2 31
3 32
4 33
5 34
EASE OF ACCESS
GRADE 1 35
2 36
3 37
4 38
5 39
6 40
7 41
DESIGNATED COUNTRYSIDE 42
GUARDIANSHIP AREAS 43
FORTS AND FORTLETS 44
OLD KILPAT. ▼
DUNTOCHER ▼
CASTLEHILL ▼
NEW KILPATRICK (BEARSDEN) ▼
BALMUILDY ▼
WILD
URBAN AREAS 45
OLD KILPATRICK
DUNTOCHER
BEARSDEN
TOTAL WITHIN URBAN AREAS 46
TOTAL OUTWITH URBAN AREAS 47
TOTAL BURIED UNDER ARTIFACTS 48
TOTAL IN OPEN LAND 49
BURIED UNDER ARTIFACTS
INDIVIDUAL LAND USES
UNDER BUILDINGS AND THEIR PRECINCTS 50
UNDER SURFACED ROADS 51
UNDER RAILWAYS 52
UNDER CANALS 53
UNDER HEAPS AND TIPS 54
UNDER QUARRIES 55
UNDER VEHICULAR UNMETALLED ROADS 56
UNDER CEMETERIES 57
IN OPEN LAND
INDIVIDUAL LAND USES
IN CULTIVATED AGRICULTURE (ARABLE & GRASS) 58
IN ROUGH GRAZINGS 59
IN MARKET GARDENS AND NURSERIES 60
IN PRIVATE OPEN SPACE 61
IN PUBLIC OPEN SPACE 62
IN DERELICT AND UNUSED LAND 63
IN GOLF COURSES 64
IN PLANTED WOODLAND 65
IN SEMI-NATURAL WOODLAND 66
37 36 35 34 33 32 31 30 29 28

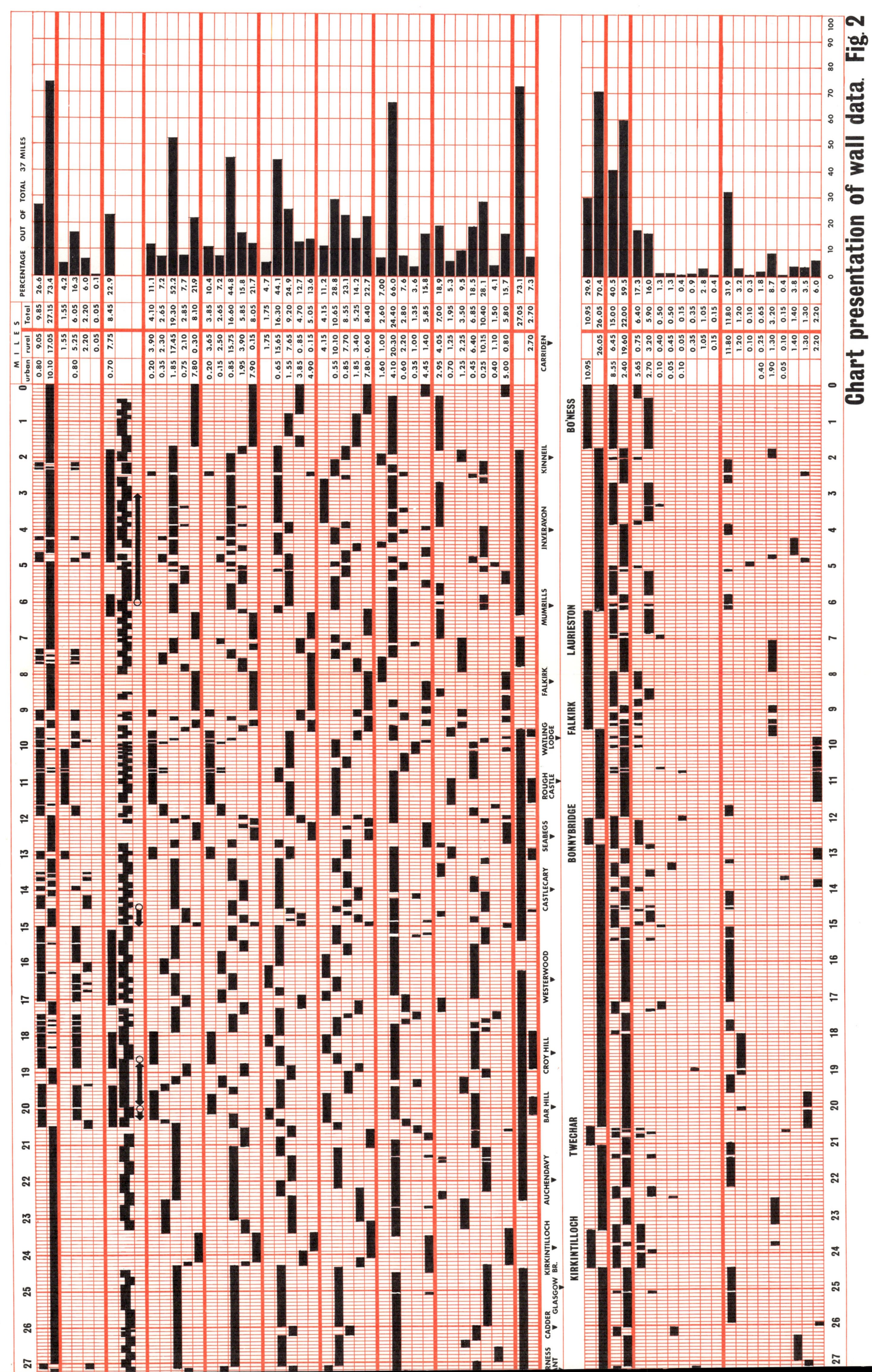

Chart presentation of wall data. Fig 2

A number of points emerge from a glance at the general pattern of the chart and the percentage columns on the right-hand side, on which some comment will be useful in establishing the present condition of the Wall and its surroundings.

In giving a detailed description of the Wall and its surroundings, the use of Fort names and Town names, which are given in lines 44 and 45, is no longer adequate in locating particular features, and these will now be identified by their mileage along the Wall (starting from the east), with an additional place name where possible.

Visible Evidence of Roman Work

Wall in the first three categories of appearance described on page 9 and shown in lines 3-6 of Figure 2 accounts for 26.6% or 9.85 miles of the line, of which over 9.0 miles is outside built-up areas. Of this only 2.2 miles is in grade 3, which gives us 7.65 miles of Wall line with clear visible traces.

Lines 1 and 2 of the chart show very clearly the great preponderance of invisible Wall west of Twechar or M 20.5, Wall in grade 2 being found only in four short lengths, totalling half a mile in all in this stretch, with no Wall in grade 1 at all. At the eastern end there are scattered short lengths of well-defined Ditch as far as Watling Lodge or M 9.0, just west of Falkirk, after which a stretch of $11\frac{1}{2}$ miles begins within which is the greatest concentration of clear remains, including the two visible Forts, with quite long continuous Wall sections in grades 1 and 2.

As far as clear visible remains are concerned, there is an overwhelming concentration of these between Falkirk and Twechar, a scattering to the east, and rare isolated sections to the west.

Immediate Surroundings of the Wall

In describing the character of the immediate surroundings of the Wall conventional ideas of what constitutes a good landscape are not wholly appropriate. There is so much difficulty for the layman in conjuring up a mental image of what the Wall once was that the landscape which is most appropriate will not be the neatly cultivated Park or the well tended golf course. The ideal ground would be where there is a clearly defined escarpment north of the Wall with rough grazing or similar land immediately at the Wall. Were there any location where the northerly ground was forested after an interval of a quarter of a mile or so of rough grazing, this might be considered as the perfect setting for reconstructing a mental image of the function and strategic siting of the Wall in Roman times.

Line 7 of Figure 2 shows the lengths in which there is a clearly defined escarpment, and Line 59 shows the lengths in rough grazings. None of the ground gives a dense forest to the north except at Rough Castle, where it is too close, and does not help to establish the idea of the frontier. At other locations where there is woodland it is also more obstructive than helpful to the aspect now being discussed, as between Bo'ness and Inveravon where the woods obscure the northward view and also the escarpment, and at Bar Hill where the Wall goes through a cut between woodlands, coniferous forest to the south and deciduous to the north.

However, woodlands are not necessarily detractions, but can help in other ways; their function in allowing the Wall line to be picked out at a distance has already been mentioned, and there are places where they serve to insulate the Wall from distracting outside modern development and place it in a small world of its own in which the imagination might conceivably work better than in more authentic but less peaceful surroundings. Such parts are found at Seabegs Wood and at Tentfield*, and in general, trees adjacent to the Wall are an improvement rather than a detraction, taking all points of view into consideration.

The ranking of the appearance of the surroundings in five grades is covered in lines 10-19 of Figure 2; lines 10-14 deal with the most important northward views towards the barbarians, while lines 15-19 deal with the southern view. To the north the aspects of strategic defence are important; to the south the requirements of appearance are less demanding.

Tentfield lies between Rough Castle and Falkirk.

PLATE SIX: The line of the Wall descending to the Clyde with no visible trace   Grade 5   (see page 12)

Grade 1, lines 10 and 15, comprise semi-natural woodland, scrub, heath and rough grass.

Grade 2, lines 11 and 16, comprise the same but interspersed with elements of cultivation of either farmland or forestry.

Grade 3, lines 12 and 17, comprise more strongly cultivated environments, farming, golf courses, and parkland.

Grade 4, lines 13 and 18, represent a rural/urban mixture, farmland plus artifacts, urban fringes, church yards and major roads.

Grade 5, lines 14 and 19, are unrelieved urban and industrial areas.

Figure 2 shows at once that both to north and south the immediate surroundings of the Wall fall more into grade 3 than into any other, and after that grade 5 is the most frequently found. 10.5% (average of north and south) is found to be in rough grazings, heath and semi-natural woodlands, which is grade 1, and these stretches also, as might be expected, coincide to a marked degree with areas where the visible remains are good, as the more cultivated sections of farmland have naturally been more destructive. Attention is thus once more brought on to the Croy Hill, Bar Hill and Rough Castle sections.

Views to More Distant Countryside

The longer views out from the Wall also have some importance in this general description of the Wall and its "corridor." There are no outstanding viewpoints to beautiful country, with the possible exceptions of views from Croy Hill and Bar Hill, but there are many pleasing long views to a horizon of hills, over a variety of mixed foregrounds, views which are valuable due to their open spaciousness. Like the other factors so far described, the character of view varies markedly at different sections of the Wall, and these also have been categorised on a similar system of five grades and ten lines, five for northward views and five for southward (lines 20-29 of Figure 2).

The grades are defined as follows:

Grade 1 Lines 20 and 25. Views open, no significant artifacts.

Grade 2 Lines 21 and 26. Views partially obscured, no significant artifacts, *or* Views open with some artifacts.

Grade 3 Lines 22 and 27. Views open, extensive significant artifacts, *or* Views partially obscured, some significant artifacts, *or* Views wholly obscured, no significant artifacts.

Grade 4 Lines 23 and 28. Views partially obscured, extensive significant artifacts, *or* Views wholly obscured, some significant artifacts.

Grade 5 Lines 24 and 29. Views wholly obscured, extensive significant artifacts.

It is recognised that this cumbersome definition of views may serve to put many readers of this study off the task of following this description any further, but if something more precise is required than just a statement that the Wall runs the gamut of the possible landscape types and their mixtures as found in the Scottish Central Belt then a method has to be found of pinning down the factors about which there is likely to be controversy. The principal factor is the amount of development, or construction of artifacts, which the outlook from the Wall contains, combined with the freedom of view which is afforded. Where the views are marked as open to the north it may be assumed in all cases that the far horizon is bounded by hills, sometimes further away, sometimes nearer, and that the foreground will be in agriculture or in built-up area or a mixture of both.

It would require many photographs to do justice to the changing character of these views out from the Wall, but four are included in Plates 7 and 8 which give some idea of the relation of the Wall above its escarpment to the carse floor opposite Grangemouth in the east, and of the character of the hills to the north in the central and western sections.

Plate 7a. A view over the carse to Grangemouth, showing the heavily industrialised middle distance. The hills north of the Forth are so far away as to be only a faint backdrop, often invisible. A good sense of the Roman Frontier is obtained in spite of the industry, as it is well below the Wall.

PLATE SEVEN (A): View from the Wall towards Grangemouth

PLATE SEVEN (B): View from the Wall to the Kilsyth Hills near Kirkintilloch

Plate 7b. A view from near Kirkintilloch north towards the Kilsyth hills which shows them much as they are seen from the Wall for the whole length between Castlecary and Kirkintilloch.

Plate 8a. A view from Wilderness Plantation towards the better wooded, more productive farming country to be found in this section. As near Kirkintilloch, the middle distance continues to have a sprinkling of built development, and this is characteristic of the views from the Wall except for the short distance of 1.75 miles shown in Line 20 of Figure 2.

Plate 8b. A view towards the much closer Kilpatrick Hills at the extreme west end of the Wall where there are no buildings in the view and the hillsides are much steeper.

Few of the artifacts in the views themselves have any contribution to make to enhancing the landscape, with the possible exception of the refinery at Grangemouth, for the viewing of which the Wall line offers a grandstand position. The tar distillery at Watling Lodge is also felt by some to have a kind of grim beauty, but this will no doubt be a minority taste.

Views to the south, when open, are always over comparatively low ground: the Pentlands are not seen, and the prospect is often pleasant but unexciting. Callendar House is glimpsed on the south side, Polmont Church is a minor landmark, Kinneil House a pleasant structure, but little else of architectural value catches the eye. Particular detractions are the fishmeal factory and the fireclay works near Rough Castle, the first as much for its nauseating smell as for its appearance. These intrude in an area otherwise scoring at the top level on most counts, and the fishmeal smell is a severe blight on the recreational prospects.

There are more completely open views to the south without artifacts than to the north, but as might be expected when open views as a whole, including artifacts, are considered the northward direction is shown to be the more open and important as far as the character of the Wall is concerned, almost 50% of the Wall length lying in the top two categories, but 90%

of that 50% having a good sprinkling of built development or else some partial obscuring feature.

The canal is not a very significant component of the views from the line of the Wall except where crossings of it are made, when there is a brief connection. An exception to this is in the Crow Hill—Bar Hill stretch, where the canal appears in plan from high on these hills, but there is of course no physical contact between it and the Wall when seen from these points.

Ease of Walking Along the Wall

Lines 30-34 show the ease of walking along the Wall line from the point of view of the physical nature of the terrain.

As before, five grades have proved a good basis for classification, as follows:

Grade 1 Line 30. Very easy. Mown grass, or short grass (grazed), no very steep land, no fences or a few easy fences; tracks and distinct footpaths, quiet roads (unclassified) (private and public).

Grade 2 Line 31. Moderately easy. Agricultural land with few fences, churchyards, public roads, open woodland without field layers.

Grade 3 Line 32. Moderately difficult. Woodland with fairly heavy field layers, agricultural land with frequent fences, steep or wet land.

Grade 4 Line 33. Very difficult. Woodland with dense field layers, difficult to penetrate, high fences, very steep land, tips and dumps.

Grade 5 Line 34. Impossible. Buildings, motorways, general urban areas.

As the summary shows, most of the Wall is in the "moderately easy" category (66%), and the next most frequent category is "impossible", with 15.8%.

Access to the Wall

Lines 35-41 of Figure 2 deal with ease of access as follows:

Line 35 Wall line under a public road—full accessibility.

PLATE EIGHT (A): View from the Wall to the Kilsyth Hills north of Wilderness Plantation

PLATE EIGHT (B): View from the western end of the Wall towards the Kilpatrick Hills

Line 36 Wall line with invitation to the public to walk; DoE notices and footways, reasonably easy to walk along.

Line 37 Wall line with informal invitation to walk; public open space without footpaths along the Wall line, or private land with a clearly marked footpath along the Wall line.

Line 38 Wall line with no invitation to walk but no obvious deterrents; rough grazings, unfenced woodlands etc.

Line 39 Wall line in fenced land in agriculture, no particular difficulty of passage, but no invitation to enter.

Line 40 Wall line with formal deterrents to access; private notices, unclimbable fences, private gardens etc.

Line 41 Access impossible; motorways, built-up etc.

As the pattern of the lines shows, this aspect of the Wall is as fragmented as any other, there being 101 different sections when classified by accessibility as described above.

Some of these sections require further explanation, in order to get a picture of access conditions along the Wall in more detail than is provided by Figure 2 alone. A number of the points described here are also illustrated in Plates 9 and 10. Where a (9) or (10) is shown in the paragraphs below an illustration can be found under the appropriate mileage distance on one of these Plates.

Beyond M1. 75 lie Kinneil House Grounds (9), where there is a pattern of footpaths already, but as the line of the Wall is invisible there is no acknowledgement of it in the lay-out of the park. At M 2.05 the House Grounds give way to cultivated land, but this land is in fact owned by the Local Authority and let to a tenant farmer, so there is no impediment to creating further access, and there are remains of the Ditch in these fields. The small neck of woodland beyond the cultivated fields is also in public ownership, and is an arm of the House Grounds traversed earlier. Beyond this is further cultivation which has no visible remains,

and which is not owned by the Council, up to M 2.7 (10). This section between M 1.75 and 2.7 is isolated by sections under public roads to east and west, but there is scope within that mile length for a better exploitation of the Wall remains. The existing fact of public ownership should permit better public display of the Wall and scope for recreation generally.

Between M 3.75 at the River Avon and 5.15 at Polmont there is a confused section which also contains land in public ownership and some of the Ditch in fair preservation, in a location where it is well seen, climbing a hillside. Public roads run close to the first part of this section, which is through cultivated land down to the Avon River where, there being no bridge, no progress could anyway be made along the exact Wall line. Beyond the Avon, Grangemouth Town Council are operating a ski slope close to the Wall in the section where the Ditch is distinct (9), and as soon as this hazard is passed the Wall line traverses a golf course under construction. Here the Department of the Environment is in consultation with the Town Council, whose golf course it is, and tees and greens are being negotiated in positions off the Wall line; however, public access to the Wall for recreation is not really maintained, as the game will be played across the Wall line and the walker along the Wall would be interfering with the primary land use. The golf course ends around M 4.7, but from 4.4 onwards the line of the Wall is thought to fall under two large reservoir tanks on the southern perimeter of the golf course. The access conditions here are a little easier, as walking along the golf course perimeter is less of a problem than picking a way through the middle of the course. At M 4.8 a coniferous woodland contains clear remains of the Ditch. This woodland is an important landmark in picking out the Wall line from a distance (10). At M 4.9 there is a tree nursery owned by Stirling County Council, in which the Wall line is seen crossing a pronounced hillock. After a cemetery and an agricultural field further progress is halted by the Motorway at M 5.15 (10).

The Wall line next emerges from under the motorway and associated roads at M 5.8, where it lies in a cultivated field close to the road as far as M 6.2, with nothing to be seen.

Having passed the Burgh of Laurieston there is 0.9 miles of easily accessible Wall line in which there are several clearly visible sections of Ditch in the Callendar Estate grounds (10). Here housing stands just back from the Wall line, which lies in a park-like setting. There are no footpaths, and the casual passer-by is unlikely to guess that the Ditch has any Roman connections. This condition continues between M 7.0 and M 7.9.

At M 9.0 the Wall line has been preserved from being built over by a recent development which nevertheless hems it in tightly on both sides for most of its short length up to M 9.2. There is general public access to the preserved section where the Ditch is well defined (9). Another small section of Wall line remains in public open space surrounding new housing development between M 9.35 and M 9.5, but it is hard to imagine the line of the Wall, which either skirts or is covered by an adjacent factory at one point (10).

Leaving Falkirk, from M 9.5 onwards the first invitation to the public to view the Wall is found, as far as M 9.75, where progress is squarely blocked by Watling Lodge, built on the line of the Wall, and the walker has no choice but to return the way he came. In this section the Wall is in grade 1. Beyond this building the remains continue visible, but there is no public access and the dense undergrowth would anyway make progress difficult as far as the minor road which crosses the Wall at M 9.85. After that the line continues through private semi-natural woodland where walking is not too difficult (9). Buildings again block the way at M 10.05 to 10.15, after which the same character continues (9), and with a few minor obstacles, such as the mineral railway, reaches the National Trust for Scotland property at Rough Castle, where there is invited public access from M 10.9 to M 11.6, and some of the best preserved remains of the Wall (10).

The section from M 9.5 to M 10.9 represents one in which efforts to remove difficulties or circumnavigate obstacles by proper detour paths would show a good return for effort, both in enhancing the existing facilities at Watling Lodge and Rough Castle and in opening up more lengths of Wall in a section where there are good remains to be seen.

The National Trust for Scotland property ends at M 11.6, where the Wall line enters the walled grounds of Bonnyside House, after which it traverses rough grass fields and then further progress is halted by the railway, a rubbish tip and the outskirts of Bonnybridge (10). The section from M 9.5 to M 11.9 can be thought of as all being made capable of ready access, but a walker along the Wall finds himself forced into a housing estate at M 11.9, or else must retrace his steps.

From Bonnybridge as far as the A 80 trunk road is another confused section, M 12.7 to M 14.9, in which the Wall line dodges under roads and the canal, through a bowling green and through cultivated fields where it is nominally visible. The section does, however, contain Seabegs Wood, M 12.8 to M 13.1 (9), where the remains are in grade 1 and the Military Way is visible. Unfortunately access connections with Seabegs Wood to east and west are under public roads, making it something of an isolated port of call rather than an integrated part of the whole. The prospects of linking the various parts of this section are not good, and the idea of the Wall line is hard to maintain in the face of the frequent interruptions. A link to the Cumbernauld section is out of the question due to the intervention of the dual carriageway A 80 in a deep cutting, and a link to the Rough Castle section cannot avoid suburban Bonnybridge.

Beyond the A 80 the Wall line traverses a factory grounds (9), but the Military Way diverts from the Wall and passes the factory to the south. If this line is taken there is no difficulty and although there are some cultivated fields ahead at present in private ownership, the whole Wall line will eventually fall within Cumbernauld New Town boundary as far as M 17.1, and any obstacles which at present exist will disappear. The Ditch remains clearly distinct through much of the M 15 to M 17.1 section (10). A small diversion from the Wall line is required to get under the railway at M 17.1, and again to get around East Dullatur House at M 17.35-17.6.

From M 17.6 to M 17.9 are arable fields, through which the Wall line is visible as a wide depression (10). A pathway through this short section would probably be hard to negotiate, but it is an obvious need if the M 15 to M 17.1 section is to be linked with the other sections with good access prospects which now begin.

The section M 17.9 to M 19.2 takes in Croy Hill, which is rough grazing (9). At present there is not a right of way, to the eastern end, but the public can easily walk up from the village of Croy. Just beyond Croy starting at M 19.35 is some farming land through which the Wall line runs, but which may be easily by-passed by a small detour on the public road.

From M 19.6 on there is a clear track which lies between woodlands (9) from M 19.75 to M 20.4 and leads on to the village of Twechar at M 20.6. Rough grass land beyond Twechar is of indeterminate use, and has been shown in Figure 2 as partly agricultural and partly private open space. The canal crosses the Wall at M 21.1, cutting off further progress along the line, and making the section beyond Twechar a *cul-de-sac.*

From the canal crossing to M 22.2 the Wall line runs through agricultural fields close to, and roughly parallel with, a public road which crosses it several times (10). It is not easy to imagine the Wall line and there seems no advantage in trying to follow the Wall in these fields.

The Wall line recrosses the Canal at M 22.45, after which its line is preserved within public open space into Kirkintilloch as far as M 23.2 (10). This is not a *cul-de-sac* when walking out from Kirkintilloch, because when the canal is reached an underpass allows the walker to gain the northern, or tow-path, side of the canal a few hundred metres east of the Wall line, after which it continues as a canal-side public walk not connected with the Wall line.

Between the west side of Kirkintilloch at M 24.4 and M 25.0 the Wall line runs through fine agricultural fields (9), again not far from a parallel public road, but too far this time to have much connection with it. Beyond M 25.0 to M 25.75, however, the distance from the public road narrows until they are running side by side. In none of this section would there appear to be any point in walking on the actual line of the Wall. In part the A 803 has a public

footpath along it already, and any improvement for walkers appears most appropriate as part of future road works.

From M 25.75 the Wall line leaves the A road line and strikes across country towards Bears-den, encountering difficulties of movement along the line almost all the way (9), the only unobstructed sections being where sand quar-ries have removed the actual Wall remains but left clear parts which will eventually be infilled. M 26.6 to M 27.0 is Cawder Golf Course, where access is not possible.

Most of the rest of the Wall line as far as New Kilpatrick Cemetery at M 30.3 is through agricultural land, with short stretches of track or road in some parts, but not enough to be very useful for following the Wall. Connecting up these easy access sections would not be simple. The Kelvin is not bridged at the Wall line, an abandoned railway also crosses it in a cutting, and it goes directly through the main buildings of Summerston Farm at M 28.7 (9). The Wall is invisible all the way, and the route does not provide a link between settlements or any other inducement than the line of the Wall to encourage its use. However, Crow Hill lies in this section (9 and 10) and is one of the places from which there is a fine prospect along the Wall, and between M 29 and M 30 a good deal of the Wall line is not far from field boundaries, which gives a better prospect of negotiating official access; but on the whole it is the least promising section of the Wall within Designated Countryside* in respect of encouraging future public visitation or use.

The Wall line is seen in isolated small sections in Bearsden, but the route of it cannot be very easily followed from one to the other (9). Leaving Bearsden the section M 32.2 to 32.5 leading up to Castlehill is a public walkway left along the Wall line, with housing on either side. From M 32.5 to 33.3 the Wall line runs through agricultural land, partly along fence lines before reaching an unsurfaced road which follows it almost to Duntocher (10). This farmland has a doubtful future, as it is a com-paratively small area almost surrounded by housing estates, and it should not be hard to arrange a public walkway the full distance from Bearsden to Duntocher (9). In Duntocher the Wall line is briefly accessible on Golden

*Designated Countryside refers to Designation under Section 2 of the Countryside (Scotland) Act 1967, and is shown at Line 42 of Figure 2 in relation to the Wall.

Hill in a public park at M 34.4-34.6 (10), and leaving Duntocher there is a well-used track through the fields which leads the walker along the Wall from M 35.5 to 35.8, and then climbs up the hillside to the north, leaving the Wall line (10). From M 35.8 onwards any walk along the Wall line which could be negotiated through the farmland would inevitably be a *cul-de-sac*, as progress is completely halted by the dual carriageway road at M 36.6, and after that the built-up area of Old Kilpatrick completes the distance to the Clyde at M 37.0 (9).

Proposals for walking routes are dealt with in Chapter 6, but following this description of the access situation a brief summary of the main opportunities and difficulties which are presented can be made.

M 1.75-2.7 A section including a public park in which immediate improvements could be made to display and use the Wall line, but from which further walkways to east and west can only be along public roads.

M 3.75-5.15 A section including enough publicly owned land to warrant looking at ways and means of making better sense of, and access to, the Wall line through all the land uses of the section; but no way in which it can easily be joined to neighbouring sections.

M 7.0-7.9 No access problems, but the lack of display or real acknowledgement of the existence of the Wall could be remedied. No possibility of connections to neighbouring sections.

M 9.5 -11.9 Connections between already accessible parts could be achieved here and an official public route established.

M 12.7-14.9 There seems little prospect of joining together the disparate sections of this stretch, nor of organising any links with neighbouring sections.

M 15.0-17.1 Where there are at present obstacles in this section they are likely to disappear soon.

M 17.1-17.9 An important part through which to gain access, in order to link through between neighbouring easy sections, but one where this will possibly be difficult.

M 17.9-21.1 Passage is already easy through ground in the Guardianship of the Department of the Environment.

West of M 21.1 agriculture and other obstacles cause increasing difficulties of access, and there is less justification for putting a linear footpath high on the list of priorities. There are, however, some obvious opportunities.

M 29.6 Access might be gained to the top of Crow Hill from where the outlook is very fine.

M 32.2-34.1 A public footpath along the line of the Wall could be negotiated from Bearsden to Duntocher.

Land Use

Lines 46-49 of Figure 2 give a good impression of the relation of the Wall line to existing development.

Line 42 shows that 29.6% of the Wall is in built-up areas, while 73% is in Designated Countryside. Comparison with Line 48 shows that the built-up areas contain frequent open spaces, while comparison with Line 1 shows hat these quite frequently have visible remains. The total length of Wall under artifacts is very much greater than the length in built-up areas, being 40.5% of the whole.

Of this, as might be expected, buildings, Line 50, and surfaced roads, Line 51, together account for 33 of the 40.5%. The remainder is under railways, canals, heaps and tips, quarries, unmetalled roads and cemeteries, as illustrated in Lines 52-57. Where roads, railways and the canal cross the Wall they cover too little land to be measurable on the chart, and lengths shown under these categories are where the Wall is covered for a distance by a road, railway or canal running parallel, or nearly so, with the line of the Wall. Motorways are wide enough to show even when crossing at right angles.

Lines 58-66 deal with the uses of the open land, of which by far the largest quantity is in cultivated and grass fields, the percentage in this category being 31.9 of the whole Wall length. This, however, is a remarkably low figure when it is realised that other open space uses add up to 27.7% of the total.

The grades of agricultural value established by the Ministry of Agriculture are not mapped on any of the maps in this study, as information was not available continuously over the whole length of the Wall, and such information as does exist was widely scattered and to collate it would have involved an amount of effort disproportionate to its likely usefulness.

The Cumbernauld extension will in the future cut out the agricultural land use between M 15 and M 17, which is at present the longest unbroken stretch in agriculture, and when this has happened agriculture will be only a minor factor in terms of quantity along the Wall line east of M 17. Other takeovers of agricultural land in favour of recreation are expected to make inroads on the farmland west of M 17, so that even in the more agricultural west it is also likely to be in decline as a factor along the Wall. These changes will be discussed in more detail in the section of the study dealing with existing recreation proposals.

Line 59. Rough grazings are concentrated at Croy Hill, where there is already guaranteed public access.

Line 60. Market Gardens and Nurseries includes the Stirling County Council tree nursery.

Line 61. Private Open Space includes the grounds of substantial properties which could hardly be described as built-up areas. These are mostly residential property, but an exception is the College of Education which occupies part of the Callen-

dar Estate through whose grounds the Wall goes.

Line 62. Public Open Space comprises some public parks, but also a number of spaces whose only use is to contain the Wall line where planning restrictions have saved it from development. These sometimes have walkways, but in other cases are just gaps in development. Where these spaces are wooded they are not included in semi-natural woodlands.

Line 63. This shows two small areas of apparently unused land, one at Twechar and another between the road and the canal where it is too narrow to be usable.

Line 64. The wall crosses or skirts golf courses of widely differing appearance. Polmont, M 4.5, is under construction; Keir, M 26.5, is a flat course with geometrically laid out poplar trees; Cawder, M 26.7, is a course in an old estate with magnificent trees, and Douglas Park, M 30.1, is traversed by the Wall through a dense tree belt, so that the playing part of the course is virtually unseen from it.

Line 65. The planted woodlands are principally on Bar Hill, but small areas are to be found scattered, the most important being at M 2.4 and M 4.8. The former is part of a public park, but has the character of a dense woodland with little access, and is therefore included in this category.

Line 66. This shows semi-natural woodland, the bulk of which is to be found at or near Rough Castle and Seabegs Wood.

The 27.7% of the Wall which is in open space other than agricultural fields has no dominant component of use, all the uses being of small extent, but taken together they have an important effect on the character of the Wall overall, and contribute to its highly fragmented appearance, which shows on the chart as 135 changes of use over the 37 mile length.

IMPLEMENTATION OF THE SURVEY PART OF THE BRIEF

The brief for this study requires a Survey of the line of the Wall and its landscape corridor, paying particular regard to:

1. Adjacent landforms and land uses

2. Areas of scientific interest

3. Areas where there is an existing public interest in the land

4. Significant visual features within the corridor.

1. Adjacent Landforms and Land Uses

This factor is complex and not easily covered in a single plan, so that the information has had to be covered by a combination of Plates 7, 8, 9 and 10, Figure 2, Maps Nos. 1 and 4 and the text of Chapters 2 and 3. In particular, Map No. 1 covers land use in the Wall zone, Figure 2 Line 7 describes the escarpment feature which is the principal adjacent landform to the Wall, Line 8 describes the views along the Wall, and Lines 9-18 are strictly to do with views rather than landform, but in practice, when taken in conjunction with the folded map in the rear pocket of the report, which clearly shows the limits of the surrounding watersheds by contouring, give the relation of the Wall to its surrounding topography as shown on that map.

2. Areas of Scientific Interest

There are only three areas in which scientific interest has been noted, all close to, but none on, the Wall. These are:

(a) Wilderness Plantation, close to the Fort of the same name, is a Site of Special Scientific Interest noted by the Nature Conservancy under Section 23 of the National Parks and Access to the Countryside Act 1949.

(b) Woodlands in the Avon valley near Inveravon Fort, which are about to be notified officially as a Site of Special Scientific Interest.

(c) Woodlands at Rough Castle in which the Nature Conservancy have expressed an interest, but which are not of sufficient scientific interest to make them worthy of designation as a Site of Special Scientific Interest.

Wilderness Plantation and Inveravon are unaffected by proposals for the Wall zone, but the woods at Rough Castle are at the centre of conflicts about landscape character and mineral exploitation which are discussed further in Chapters 5 and 7. In addition, various studies have been made of the flora and fauna of stretches of the canal, but in general the canal is not likely to play a great part in development concerning the Wall specifically, although it may be very important within the Country Park proposals which include it within their boundaries, and therefore any further consideration of this factor will appropriately form part of studies into the organisation of these Country Parks.

3. Areas where there is an Existing Public Interest in the Land

The principal and obvious public landholdings are described in Chapter 6, in addition to the comments in this chapter, and these descriptions are considered to give the main opportunities which arise from existing public landholdings for the general purposes of this study.

4. Significant Visual Features within the Corridor

The significant visual features of the Wall corridor other than those connected with the landform, which aspect has already been covered, are rather few. Some comments on this aspect will be found under the sections of Chapter 2 entitled "The Identification of the Wall in the Landscape" and "Views to more distant Countryside", and Map 2 shows their location.

SUMMARY

The analysis of the appearance of the Wall today as presented in Figure 2 underlines the fragmented character of the Wall environment, with 135 changes of use and over 100 changes of degree of accessibility within the 40% of the length which remains in open land.

This means that there can be no easy description of the Wall corridor, as it has no constant character for more than short stretches, and it means that in formulating proposals bold strategies of zonation will be only a background to the real front of activity, which will be concerned with the many large and small scale impacts and opportunities which will arise continuously within these many sections of the Wall environment.

4 the existing protection of the wall and its environment

Methods of Protection

The Wall and its environment may be protected at present by

1. The Secretary of State acting through the Department of the Environment, or the Local Authority under Acts dealing with Ancient Monuments (1882, 1914, 1931 and 1953).

2. The Local Planning Authority under the Planning Acts.

3. The Owners of the land as a matter of policy.

4. Land Uses unconnected with Ancient Monuments but accidentally protecting them.

In practice, the Local Authorities have seldom, if ever, used their powers under the Ancient Monuments Acts, and for practical purposes the whole duty to take action under them is shouldered by the Secretary of State.

1. The Ancient Monuments Acts

The means which the Acts place at the disposal of the Department are:—

(a) Powers to purchase and own Monuments. Only a short length beside the Antonine Wall is owned by the Secretary of State at Watling Lodge, and forms a buffer zone which was purchased to keep nearby housing back from the Wall (not owned by the Secretary of State).

(b) Guardianship Agreements. These imply a contract between the Owner and the Secretary of State allowing him to maintain the Monument and forbidding the Owner from damaging it. The agreement is in perpetuity and binding even if the land is sold.

In practice, Guardianship Agreements ensure public access to the Monument, for which the Secretary of State has the right to charge if he so wishes, but the Act does not make public access an obligatory part of any Guardianship Agreement. There are no entry charges to Guardianship areas on the Antonine Wall.

There are four miles of the Wall and four Forts in Guardianship. Guardianship Agreements have in the past been entered into only for Monuments where there have been visible

Although other Authorities do not have any particular policy, and in Dunbartonshire a length of Wall including Bar Hill is not covered by any Development Plan, all show an awareness of the Wall's importance, and the Planning Committees of all the Authorities support a general protection policy. Some wish to make a more formal Development Plan protection for the Wall at their next Quinquennial Review.

The present system is that the Planning Authorities contact the Department of the Environment whenever Ancient Monuments are threatened by new zonings, and sometimes, but not always, in cases where damaging development applications are in accordance with the Development Plan. This is logical, but not as useful as it might be from the protective point of view, as modification of a scheme basically permitted by the Development Plan could be very important for the environment of the Wall. It would clearly be desirable for the Development Plan to carry a protective zone which would bring all projects affecting the Wall to the notice of the Department of the Environment.

About six miles of the Wall falls in designated Green Belt in Lanarkshire as shown on Map No. 2. The designation is on grounds unconnected with the Wall and in fact covers hardly any visible remains. The view from Crow Hill shown on Plate 10 covers the western end of the Green Belt section.

At Cadder the Secretary of State has reversed a decision of the Local Planning Authority which turned down a development proposal in the Green Belt adjacent to the Wall. This shows that the Green Belt, even where the Local Planning Authority is trying to defend it, will not always be sufficient protection, and if the environment of the Wall is to be safeguarded then a specific zoning referring to the Wall would possibly be more effective.

There have been substantial losses to development, both building and mineral extraction, along the Wall, but there have also been a number of successes where the Planning Authority has managed to protect the Wall even without a formal Development Plan protection zone.

Examples are:

(a) At Kinneil, housing has been kept back some yards from the line of the Wall, here invisible. (Plate 9).

(b) At Callendar Park multi-storey flats have been kept clear of the Wall, which is here represented by a well-defined Ditch. (Plate 10).

(c) At Bantaskine, M 9.1, a short stretch of Wall where the Ditch is well-defined forms a small public open space surrounded by houses (Plate 9).

(d) The extension of Kirkintilloch eastwards has not been allowed to encroach on the Wall line, here invisible (Plate 10).

(e) The quarrying at Croy Hill has been settled by agreement to avoid further damage to the Wall line, although prior consent for quarrying right up to the Wall exists.

(f) At Crow Hill a Glasgow Corporation proposal for housing was turned down completely, not merely set back, and the 400 foot amenity zone established in the Development Plan remains undeveloped.

(g) At Castlehill housing on either side of the Wall has been kept back, leaving a green corridor where the Wall is invisible.

Expansion of quarrying at Rough Castle is now at the negotiation stage, and it is expected that this issue will also be satisfactorily resolved.

It can therefore be said that the system is showing results, but that they are *ad hoc* adjustments and not entirely foolproof in securing protection.

Apart from seeking to ward off development, several Authorities are promoting positive development of their own to try and enhance the Wall line, but these aspects will be covered under the chapter on Existing Proposals.

3. **Ownership of the Land**

Of the seven Guardianship areas, three belong to the National Trust for Scotland (those at Watling Lodge, Rough Castle and Seabegs Wood). Although the Trust itself is a body which manages land, receives the public and interprets to them the heritage aspects of remains, and this has been a stronger criterion for their selection than their archaeological importance, but there is no reason why agreements should not be entered into when the Monument is invisible.

The present policy of the Secretary of State is to bring all visible remains of the Antonine Wall into Guardianship, and so far this has been achieved for about half the visible remains.

The present Guardianship areas are:

Watling Lodge	¼ mile
Rough Castle, including the Fort	
	3/5 mile
Seabegs Wood	¼ mile
Castlecary, including the Fort	
	short stretch
Westerwood-Twechar	1 mile approx.
Croy Hill, including the Fort	1 mile
Bar Hill, including the Fort	1/3 mile approx.

Of the visible remains still to be brought into Guardianship, the most important parts are to the east of Rough Castle, to the east of Croy Hill and to the east of Bar Hill Guardianship areas.

(c) Scheduling. Scheduling implies a statement of public interest in an Ancient Monument which obliges the Owner to notify the Secretary of State of his intention to alter, damage or remove it, and forbids him to do so for a period following the notification during which the Secretary of State or the Local Authority may decide on further protective measures.

As compensation of owners is consequent on further protection, and money has not been forthcoming for this, scheduling in practice means only a stay of execution during which time the Monument may be further investigated, if there are still thought to be archaeological interests to be followed up by its further investigation. Damage or destruction of Scheduled Monuments without prior notification is punishable by £100 fine or three months imprisonment.

About twenty two miles of the Wall, ten Forts and twelve Camps are scheduled, and this total, plus the four miles of Guardianship, is almost the whole of the Wall line outside built-up areas. Scheduling was provided for under the Act of 1882, but has proceeded only slowly, and there still remains one short stretch of the Wall which has to be scheduled.

The Acts provide for the imposition of fines for damaging or destroying an Ancient Monument, but there is no provision for its restitution after damage has been caused. Fining is not common, and the only case which has come to light during this study when a fine has been imposed has been where a householder, through whose garden the Ditch runs, constructed a rockery in it, and planted the Ditch sides with shrubs.

Appendix 1 lists all the Scheduled lengths of the Wall and Guardianship areas as at 1972, and Guardianship is further identified in Line 43 of Figure 2.

(d) Amenity Areas. The 1931 Act permits the creation of Amenity Areas in relation to Ancient Monuments, within which buildings may be restricted, altered or cleared away etc. This provision also incurs liability for compensation, so that it has not been freely used. Amenity Areas have been created in relation to Hadrian's Wall, but not in relation to the Antonine Wall. Where an Amenity Area is not being declared the area of the Monument is defined to include only such surrounding land as is required for fencing, or preserving the Monument from injury and for access to it.

2. **The Planning Acts**

The Planning Authorities along the Wall are:

West Lothian County Council
Stirling County Council
Falkirk Town Council
Lanark County Council
Dunbarton County Council
Glasgow Corporation
Clydebank Town Council

Of these, only the City of Glasgow has any specific policy towards the Wall recorded on their Development Plan over and above noticing it as a scheduled Ancient Monument. The Glasgow provision is a corridor 400 feet wide which is to be kept free of development along the one mile length of the Wall within the City boundary. It includes the important Crow Hill and part of Balmuildy Fort and its surroundings.

2. Where engineering requirements leave little choice but to do some damage to the Wall. An example of this is found at Polmont-hill, where the existing reservoir was extended into new buried tanks on the Wall line.

Lanark County Council is working on a revision of the Bishopbriggs Development Plan which may have the effect of reducing the extent of mineral consents in the zone of the Wall and of the canal north of this, but even if this improvement takes place there will still be areas of damaging mineral consented land along the Wall. For this reason and others given earlier the whole question of mineral workings should be further studied so that a better balance may be arrived at between consents, demand and total availability.

Trouble along the Wall may be expected to continue, therefore, on both these counts in the future, in spite of the new Amenity Zones. The County Development Plans contain industrial and residential zonings within the Amenity Zones which are not taken up, but which do not do serious damage to the Wall apart from those discussed in Chapter 5. The problems of prior consents now stem principally from mineral extraction.

The Form of Development Control to be Exercised

Having defined the Amenity Zones it is necessary to give an indication of what kind of control would be appropriate within them, and having shown the desirability of an Article 4 restriction of permitted development it is necessary to indicate in what areas and circumstances it should be applied.

In order to do this the Amenity Zones as proposed by the Scottish Development Department and the Department of the Environment (with small boundary adjustments to take account of building encroachment since their original definition) are proposed as the basic area of development control, and three sub-zones of the Amenity Zones are defined in which varying degrees of control are proposed. These are shown on Map No. 3. The sub-zones assume that in the first zone no development over or under the Wall itself is desirable, and that in a second zone no above-ground development near the Wall would be desirable.

Beyond that a third zone is indicated where development might be permitted provided it did not interfere with the outlook from the Wall.

It is recommended that Article 4 should be applied in sub-zones 1 and 2 only. As these form a comparatively narrow band along the Wall the effect on the workload in the Planning Offices and the inconvenience in making additional planning applications would be kept to a minimum.

The division into sub-zones takes no account of the improvement which might be effected by screening and which might allow building in sub-zone 2 in some cases. For instance, a good deal of the Cumbernauld extension might have been unbuildable in sub-zone 2 if there was no proposal for a tree belt, but with the tree belt, building there is quite acceptable. While building land remains plentiful in the central belt of Scotland there seems little point in permitting building behind tree belts in Amenity Zones unless there is some over-riding reason why the development should be in an Amenity Zone. Further comments on the circumstances in which planting enhances the Wall environment can be found in the section on The Role of Woodlands along the Wall Line.

The question of when development in sub-zone 3 does or does not detract from the view is a more difficult matter. The boundary between the sub-zones is suggested on the basis that the topography would permit a two story building with no unusual objectionable features (such as high smoke stacks or material storage yards etc.) to be sited within it without any detrimental effect. Higher buildings would require further investigation. This guide is obviously very tentative, but gives some impression of the way in which the Amenity Zones and their sub-zones might be used.

Who Should Exercise the Development Control in the Amenity Zones?

The Local Planning Authority is automatically involved, and should be required to consult with the Department of the Environment. The Countryside Commission for Scotland may wish to be involved only in the case of applications having a serious effect, and may wish to specify to the Local Authorities concerned the kind of applications, if any, which it considers should be referred to it on the basis of a study of this report. The lengths of the Wall which fall within Designated Countryside are shown at line 42 of Figure 2.

The scope of the involvement of the Scottish Development Department in development control in the Amenity Zones as at present being discussed is set out in Appendix No. 2. The Countryside Commission for Scotland may still have an interest of its own to pursue here on the recreation side, and any decision to involve itself in a proportion of cases by the Scottish Development Department will not relieve the Countryside Commission for Scotland of the necessity of defining its own interests and adding its advice to that of the Scottish Development Department and the Department of the Environment accordingly.

PROPOSALS FOR THE MOST APPROPRIATE LAND USES OF THE AREA, INCLUDING RECREATIONAL USE

The requirement to recommend the most appropriate land uses for the area, including recreational use, is here interpreted as an instruction to define what projects and policies concerning land use and recreation require the support of the Commission, or need to be initiated by the Commission. This is done under the following headings:

1. Project Areas
2. Improved Access
3. Establishing the Line of the Wall in the Countryside
4. Interpretation to the Public.

The list of specific proposals which follows repeats the earlier method of working along the Wall from east to west, and is not intended to be in order of priority.

1. Project Areas

(a) **Kinneil Park**

The Commission may wish to consider encouraging the Local Authority to extend the present boundaries of its park to include all the nearby length of the Wall, and to improve its layout so that the public may be made aware of the Wall line. The Commission may also wish to consider encouraging the establishment of an interpretation centre in the park.

(b) **Polmonthill**

The Commission may wish to initiate a study of the Wall between the River Avon and Polmont, with a view to securing space for a small car park at the east end, a walkway along the Wall line clearly delineated as such and free of golfing hazards, and the best continuation of this walkway that may be devised through Little Kerse Wood and Stirling County Council tree nursery. There is existing recreational potential in open land to the south of the golf course, paths serving which would require to be integrated. The future of the ski-slope enterprise would also need to be considered in this scheme. It is anticipated that a good deal of new planting might be involved. The sewage works by the Avon is an amenity problem which should be taken into account.

(c) **Falkirk to Bonnybridge**

The National Trust is already seeking to acquire the necessary land to allow the gaps in public access in this length to be eliminated, and the Department of the Environment is most active in this section, and well aware of its importance. Stirling County Council has suggested the possibility of a Country Park here on ground which is at present proposed for open-cast mining, and has already produced a report on the Rough Castle locality. It is a length where the landowners see development possibilities and where the Wildlife Trust has indicated a natural history interest in the woodlands. In spite of all these conflicts the present machinery appears to be resolving the situation. The establishment of a proper connection between the Watling Lodge section and Rough Castle must be regarded as one of the most obvious priorities along the whole Wall.

The Country Park proposal at present is limited to the area of the open-cast proposal, and is intended to follow that land use when the mine is worked out. There will be difficulties in defining a larger area, but ultimately it would be desirable for the park to take in all the surrounding rough woodlands and exploit one of the few locations where there is a useful link with the canal. A study is now required of the scope of this future park and the programme for its progressive implementation.

The fishmeal factory, which makes a very bad smell, is a powerful deterrent to immediate development for recreation in this area. The prospect of improving or eliminating it is not known, and it may be very difficult to do anything about it; however, it is recommended that the problem be looked into.

(d) Balmuildy to Crow Hill

Crow Hill is an outstanding viewpoint on the Wall line and is surrounded by farming land with no invited access. It is in the zone protected by the Development Plan Zoning of Glasgow Corporation. There are various fence lines in the fields around which would permit a public walkway along them with little disturbance to farming and which would allow the public to reach the hilltop.

The distance of Crow Hill from Bearsden would make a local walk of convenient length; the route chosen should take the whole journey out of Bearsden along the Wall into account. A motorway line is to cut off Bearsden from Crow Hill eventually, and the route would have to cross this on a bridge, which would also take over the existing minor road.

The location is sufficiently attractive to draw people from further away who would come in cars, particularly as there are few good ways of experiencing the Wall in the west, and this would be the section most accessible from Glasgow. A small car park could therefore be usefully provided. The position of the car park is not so obvious, as the car-borne visitor may also wish to look at Balmuildy Fort. A car park site may therefore be chosen near Temple of Boclair, from which the hill may be conveniently ascended, or near Balmuildy, or both.

Balmuildy is one of the stone built Forts which could most easily be exposed and consolidated. This, of course, would be entirely for the consideration of the Department of the Environment, but if this were done then the Crow Hill-Balmuildy section would grow greatly in importance. The nearby sites along the Kelvin are in conflicting demand for both housing and public parks, and this makes it difficult to foretell the future position in this area. Clearly, in the interests of the conservation of the Wall a park along the Kelvin which spilled over the Glasgow boundary to take in the surroundings of Balmuildy Fort would be ideal.

The road past Balmuildy Fort is narrow and winding, and cuts the corner of the Fort. Should this road be improved at any time the opportunity should be taken to regain the lost corner if possible. This Fort is also one of the few which could suitably be demarcated by tree planting.

2. Improved Access

The four project areas already mentioned above, plus the Cumbernauld Town Extension, almost complete the immediate requirements for further access to the Wall from the recreational point of view. Still missing are a proper link-up of Seabegs Wood to other sections and a route between Bearsden and Clydebank.

Seabegs is a problem area; an isolated section of well-preserved Ditch, Rampart and Military Way cut off by difficult access problems for the walker on either side, and difficult car access if it were ever to become popular. The best that can be done with it is to guard it carefully in the hope that in the fullness of time circumstances around it will change sufficiently to allow its integration with the other nominally visible remains between it and Castlecary, or that redevelopment in Bonnybridge may ultimately leave a route free for it to be connected with the Rough Castle section. A stone culvert under the canal offers the possibility of a link with the towpath side and there is an attractive woodland adjacent to the Guardianship Area which the National Trust for Scotland has acquired. The Guardianship area may be promoted by association with the recreational development of this adjacent ground.

The consolidation of Castlecary Fort is a desirable objective for a later generation to follow up, and no doubt there will still be archaeologists when railways have ceased to be important.

Between Bearsden and Clydebank is the proposed Braidfield Country Park, but there is no reason to suppose that this will be made very quickly, and therefore it will be appropriate to press ahead with access agreements in the meantime, which would allow a walk to be established roughly along the Wall line between these two places.

Elsewhere access already exists or is considered not to repay the effort which would be required to establish it. However, where roads reasonably parallel with and adjacent to the Wall exist, as between Kinneil and Inveravon, between Twechar and Cadder, and immediately west of Balmuildy, then County Surveyors could be asked to ensure that footpaths are provided along them at such time as they may in the course of the County road programme fall due for improvement, and the Commission could consider these footpaths to find suitable locations at which to provide some permanently displayed information about the Wall.

3. Establishing the Line of the Wall in the Countryside

(a) Route Markers

This is the most controversial proposal of this study, the one entailing the most time, trouble and expense, and also the most important for the future of the Wall. The aim should be to mark the Wall line in such a way that passers-by cannot fail to see it whether they are interested in the Wall or not. The best markers would probably be masts set at intervals along the Wall, and they could appropriately be topped off with a Roman eagle or some such suitable symbol. The masts should be slender and be able to stand in hedgerows without interfering with agriculture. The height of the masts may well require to vary according to their location. In some places where they are seen at close range or where they are along the edge of an existing road they need very little height, but where they are to be picked out across intervening fields a height of 7 metres would be a suitable maximum. There would be no necessity to put them at regular intervals, but sufficiently often so that as one mast is left behind another appears. Where the Ditch is well marked and the line of the Wall cannot be mistaken there is no point in over-doing it by providing masts. Their greatest importance is therefore in those lengths where the public is constantly passing on adjacent roads and there is no trace of the Wall. No detailed layout of masts has been considered,

but a rough calculation suggests that 80-100 might be required for the whole Wall length.

(b) The Role of Woodlands along the Wall Line

Attention has already been drawn in Chapter 2 to the part played by woodlands in picking out the line of the Wall, and not only the Wall, but in the case of Castlehill the Fort which is on top of it. Tree roots damage the archaeological remains underground, and so trees are not very welcome on archaeological sites except when there is certainty that no remains exist. Nevertheless, from the landscape point of view Castlehill crowned with trees is a valuable landmark on the Wall, and in principle it would be very desirable to see other Fort sites similarly distinguished, provided that the trees could be planted in a zone outwith the immediate area of the remains.

Opportunities for planting along the Wall are not very frequent, and there are drawbacks as well as advantages in the presence of trees, since the objectives of trying to preserve a notion of the original Roman frontier, of allowing views to the north and of screening off present-day artifacts are often in conflict with each other.

Figure 3a shows sections through the Wall corridor in some typical places where these conflicts occur.

(i) In Callendar Park in Falkirk there is a conifer plantation on the north side of the Wall which has no relation to the Wall, but which screens off the Falkirk built-up area from the Wall line.

(ii) At Rough Castle woodland to the north has conservation value but it obscures the view and does not help the frontier impression.

(iii) Seabegs Wood gives an interesting sense of containment from present-day intrusions, but here again the outlook to the north is hidden.

(iv) Croy is an opposite case where there is no woodland and the open hillside creates a good impression of the frontier. Quarrying threatens to approach closely to the Wall on both sides, but no screening is desirable as it would destroy the outlook.

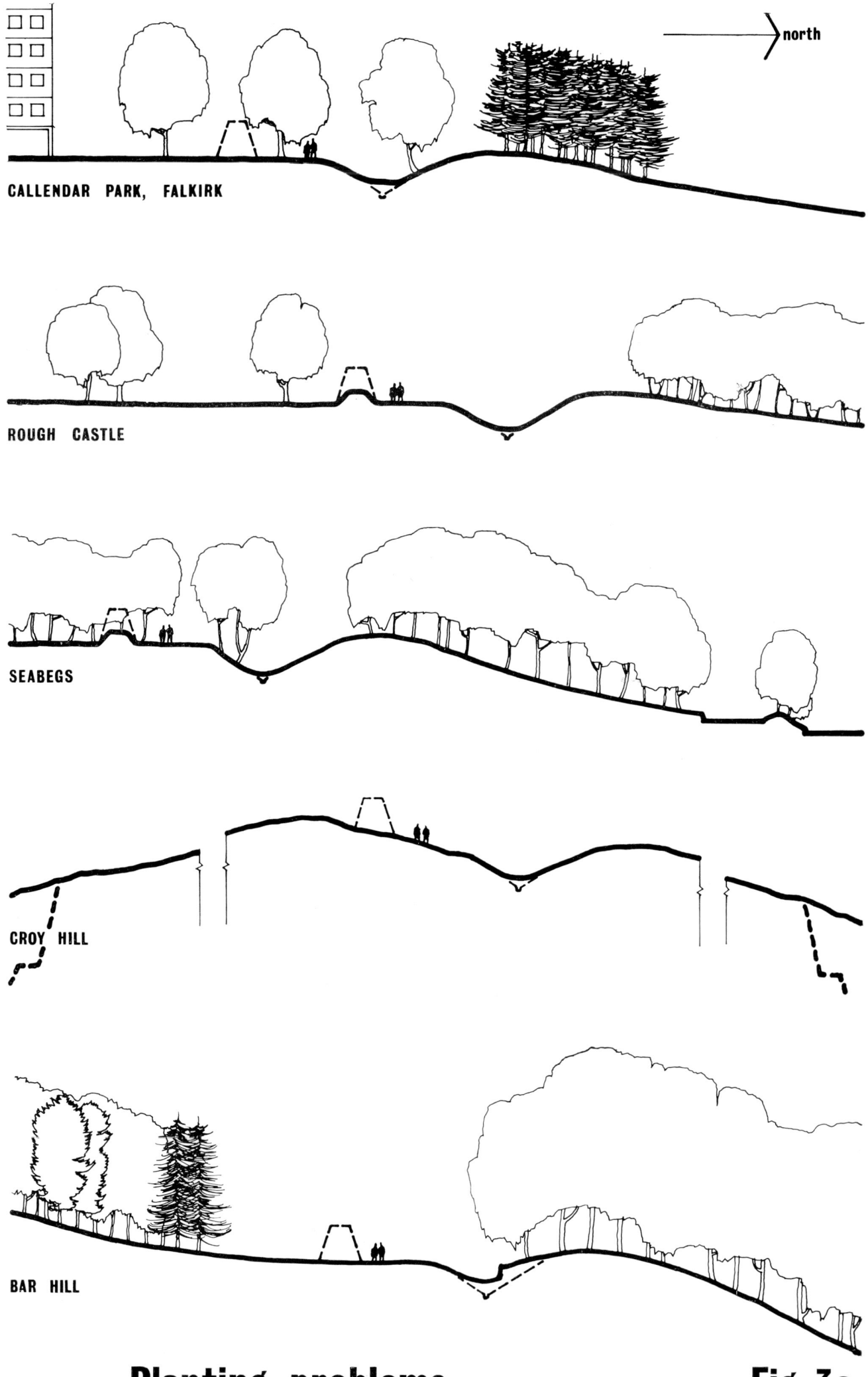

CALLENDAR PARK, FALKIRK

north

ROUGH CASTLE

SEABEGS

CROY HILL

BAR HILL

Planting problems 1:500 **Fig 3a**

(v) On Bar Hill there is a curious effect of walking in an alley between deciduous wood land on the north and conifers on the south. This emphasises the route of the Wall from a distance, but it is quite unlike the original Roman character.

(c) Planting Sites

There are a number of places where new planting to emphasise the Wall line, to screen out unpleasing views and to affirm the character of the place will be particularly appropriate. Some of these are in the proposed Project Areas, others in areas which have so far had little mention.

(i) Kinneil Park. Recent planting has not been helpful in emphasising the Wall line, and additional planting could help to rectify this.

(ii) Polmonthill. Planting is expected to play a substantial part in the co-ordination of this recreation area.

(iii) Watling Lodge (see Figure 3b). Improvement would be effected here by planting on land owned by the Secretary of State on the southern side to screen housing. The existing trees in the Ditch and on the outer mound fortunately provide a screen that will be effective in hiding future industry on the low ground to the north.

(iv) Bonnyside (see Figure 3b). Bonnyside is the western end of the Rough Castle section where there is an industrial reservoir and a lot of unpleasing building on the outskirts of Bonnybridge, the view towards which would be improved by planting a belt on the south of the Wall and in selected areas north of it. The land would have to be acquired for this. This is the only proposed planting site where there is no public interest in the land.

(v) Tollpark (see Figure 3b). Dense screen planting is necessary on the south side, but the distance between the existing industry and the Wall is not adequate to do this properly. Where the Military Way is known the planting should have been south of its line in a belt of at least 20 metres width, but this will not now be possible.

(vi) Cumbernauld Extension Area. Cumbernauld policy is to plant along the Wall in the Extension Area, but the Development Plan does not show planting all the way. The plant-ing should be considered for the whole distance, screening the views of the town to the south and leading the eye northwards over the Kelvin valley.

(vii) Westerwood (see Figure 3b). The situation of inadequate space for planting at Tollpark may be avoided at Westerwood if sufficient land, perhaps 30 metres wide, is left between the prison fence and the line of the Military Way. The section shows the approximate dimensions which would be desirable for a zone to be devoted to the Wall, a foot path and bridleway and a tree planting screen on the south side.

(viii) Twechar to Kirkintilloch (see Figure 3b). Planting belts south of the Wall are necessary at Wester Shirva if industrial expansion is permitted there. If not, then there is no call for planting. Planting on the southern edge of Queenzieburn industrial expansion is included in the Development Plan and should be carried out as soon as possible.

The last few hundred metres of the Wall as it runs into Kirkintilloch are in public open space designed to preserve the Wall. This is a featureless wide expanse of grass, and a well thought out planting plan is required, both to screen off the outskirts of Kirkintilloch on the south side of the Wall, and to make this into a pleasant recreation space. This ground is not in Designated Countryside.

(ix) Buckley. There is a proposal at Buckley, M 27.6, for an intrusion into an Amenity Zone adjacent to existing industry. The proposal is not greatly damaging to the Wall, but the opportunity can be taken to reduce the impact by screen planting.

(x) Castlehill. A similar problem arises here as at Kirkintilloch, where the Wall runs in an entirely featureless "corridor sanitaire" which it is doubtful whether the local people even know is intended to preserve the Wall line. This could be much improved with some planting in conjunction with the masts and plaques.

The cross sections shown in Figure 3b have implications from the maintenance point of view, as all the ground between the southern screen planting and the northern boundary of the Wall corridor would require some sort of

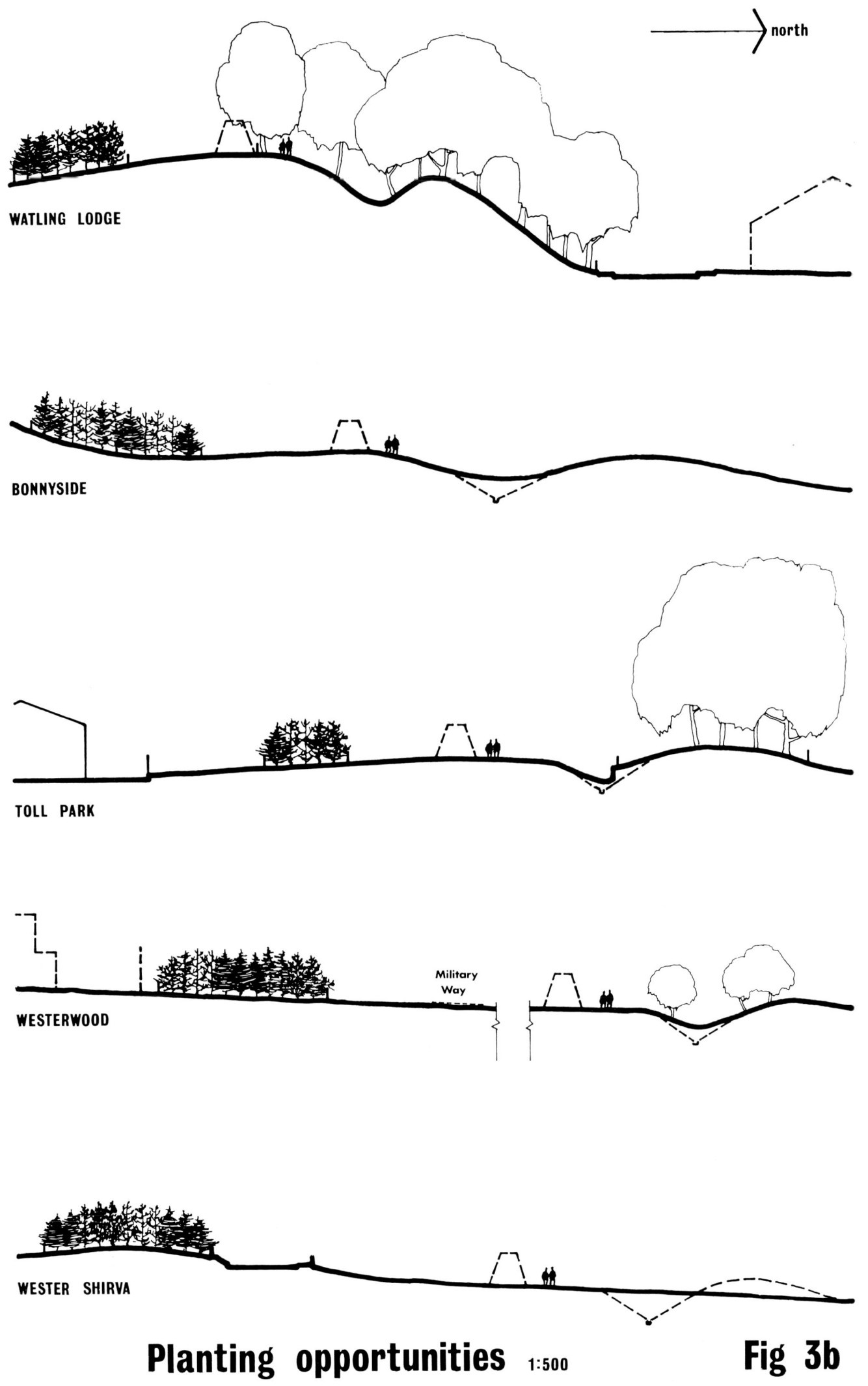

north

WATLING LODGE

BONNYSIDE

TOLL PARK

WESTERWOOD

Military Way

WESTER SHIRVA

Planting opportunities 1:500   **Fig 3b**

maintenance. Department of the Environment experience gives some guide to the problems.

The creation of a Guardianship area implies an obligation on the Department of the Environment to maintain the area. This maintenance is seen as part of an "outward expression of Guardianship". Of the four Guardianship areas only Rough Castle showed much sign of maintenance in the autumn of 1972, and gave some idea of what the character of other maintained Antonine Wall sites under more extensive Guardianship Agreements, and with more maintenance money available, might look like.

The ground at Rough Castle is scythed twice a year by a groundsman who has his permanent station on the site. Photographs taken at the original excavation of Rough Castle show the site to have been heavily wooded. Since then most of the larger trees have gone, but there is still a fair woodland cover. The scything prevents the regeneration of the woodland which is taking place outside the site boundaries with vigour. Ideally, many of the Department of the Environment staff feel that trees should be kept off the sites of the Fort, Rampart, Ditch and Military Way, and that sheep grazing would be the best maintenance.

There is a considerable amount of bracken in the Ditch at Rough Castle, and it is part of the maintenance policy to reduce this and to get a more acceptable cropped sward. The Ditch would be cleared out if funds allowed, and presumably restored to its original form, but it has proved difficult to keep the Ditch clear, at least in some parts, and it has readily returned to its former state. In addition to these attentions to the vegetation and to the erosion of the Monument itself, there are maintenance tasks associated with litter, paths, stiles, notices, fences and gates etc., as well as the reception of the public; these must all be considered when it is decided to look after the site in a manner which will encourage public access in quantities greater than just a handful of people once in a while.

For these reasons maintenance is a considerable task, and the idea is certainly not to include an immense width of land in any strip which is preserved for the Wall to run in. However, where the Military Way is known to exist the strip has to be wide enough to include it as shown in Figure 3b. The principal length where the Military Way is known is from just by the trunk road at Castlecary as far as Bar Hill, a distance which includes the whole Cumbernauld extension. Bar Hill is planted in forestry for the most part, including the zone between the Wall and the Military Way.

When the Military Way is unknown and the Department of the Environment agrees, then planting may be much closer to the Wall, as shown at Watling Lodge in Figure 3b.

(d) Accidental Wall Markers and Features on the Wall

The question of buildings on the Wall line itself leads to conflicting views between those for whom the Wall takes precedence over all other archaeological interests, so that competing items should be removed to make the Roman feeling more consistent, and others, among whom is Dr. Robertson of the Hunterian Museum, equally interested in the later accretions which mar the Roman work. Examples are old farm steadings which, standing over the Ditch, have subsided and cracked, giving evidence of the existence of the Ditch. As nothing shows above ground the removal of the steading would remove also the evidence of the existence of the Ditch. Another question arises in cases such as the mineral railway embankment across the Wall near Croy Hill, which although obscuring the Wall has itself some archaeological value.

(e) The Forth and Clyde Canal

The line of the canal follows that of the Wall for some distance and reinforces it to some extent.

Some emphasis is given to the canal in the brief for this study as a recreation opportunity linked with the Wall. Visually and physically, however, it has only a slight connection in one or two places with the Wall, and even then mostly with parts of the Wall where there are no visible remains. Exceptions to this are near Watling Lodge, where a good but densely overgrown stretch of Wall is separated from the canal by a single agricultural field zoned for industry, and also at Rough Castle, where the Wall is separated only by a semi-natural woodland; in addition there is an existing tunnel, unfortunately only 1.25 metres high, which could allow the visitor to gain the northern or towpath side of the water. At Seabegs a better tunnel joins the towpath side with a woodland adjacent to the Guardianship area where there is a good bit of Ditch remaining and the line of the Military Way is visible. Elsewhere the canal is even more divorced from the Wall except where crossings of it are made.

The canal is not a very significant component of the views from the line of the Wall except where crossings of it are made, when there is a brief connection. An exception to this is in the Croy Hill/Bar Hill stretch, where the canal appears in plan from high on these hills, but there is, of course, no physical contact between it and the Wall at these points.

4. Interpretation to the Public

The masts and such defining tree planting as exists or can be established make a statement of the line of the Wall in the public eye.

More detailed interpretation facilities will be required at particular points, and the recommendation is that there should be three of these soon, and eventually five. The exact nature of the interpretative means is a question for the Commission to consider, but the sites which are most appropriate can be selected from the background information gathered for this study.

The interpretation points should relate to the main traffic arteries, should build wherever possible on well preserved remains of the Wall in pleasant surroundings, and should be spread along the length of the Wall.

(a) Kinneil Park is a suitable location for the first of these, even though the Wall is not outstanding at this point, as it would form a suitable starting point for an enthusiast wanting to go along the whole Wall, and because it is already a very pleasant recreation area which might be enhanced by this new facility, and there are even buildings available which might house an interpretative feature.

(b) Rough Castle almost selects itself. It is the only existing part of the Wall where the motorist is invited to stop within the bounds of the area of the Monument and then to proceed through a site maintained specifically to receive him. The Wall and Fort are here preserved at their best. The Council for British Archaeology have pointed out that the Museum at Falkirk has now been closed, and that this was a local source of information about the Wall. This interpretation point could try to replace some of that local loss. Its success would depend on negotiating an extension of the Guardianship area which is too small to admit further development. Siting would have to be in the context of the overall Country Park lay-out. The danger of the loss or dispersal of the contents of the closed Falkirk Museum suggests the advisability of an early decision on this.

(c) Cumbernauld Corporation are interested in running a Wall "museum". Unfortunately it is planned to go in Cumbernauld House, which is some distance from the Wall. Cumbernauld Town Council have tried to acquire land on the Wall line from Cumbernauld Corporation for a museum; this would be better than at Cumbernauld House in that it would be related to the site, but it would not be ideally situated in the context of a general Wall strategy, being away from the better remains and unconnected with other recreational facilities. The Castlecary-Twechar stretch of the Wall should have an interpretation point, but it would be best situated outside Cumbernauld's area in the proposed park east of Kirkintilloch near Croy, in association with the network of footpaths on Bar Hill. Its siting should be considered in relation to turn-offs from the motorway which is planned to pass between Croy and Bar Hills.

(d) The situation at Balmuildy is uncertain, but if recreation other than that associated with the Wall is established by Glasgow Corporation, then Balmuildy would be a good site for the most westerly interpretation facility. If Balmuildy is largely built-up and there is little prospect of the Department of the Environment consolidating the Fort, then it may be preferable to make the westernmost interpretation point in the Castlehill/Braidfield Country Park area. Whichever is chosen eventually, this centre will be the last one to be established, due to various uncertainties.

(e) The four proposals above are for substantial interpretative features, assuming building and car park scale of provision. There is scope for many very small interpretative features, perhaps in association with the route markers already mentioned. Some sites, however, suggest something intermediate between a full centre with car park and a mere wall plaque, although it is hard to define what form such a feature would take. An instance is Callendar Park, where a good length of Ditch passes by high flat blocks which might house a small interpretative feature. These examples are not elaborated as they really do not affect planning and the Wall corridor, but opportunites for small scale interpretation features are to be found in many places along the Wall.

Some people, both archaeologists and laymen, are interested in the possibilities of rebuilding sections of the Rampart and re-opening the Ditch to restore the original appearance. The difficulties are that the original was built of turf and wood which both naturally deteriorate and are vandal prone. A concrete rampart would be not only un-authentic, but ugly and a target for spray paint; other alternatives are not easily found. The possibility might be to make the Rampart profile in the form of an open cage of steel bars over which people could climb at will but which did not attempt to reproduce the actual appearance of the original.

Dr. Robertson has suggested that the west side of Croy Hill would be a suitable place for a reconstructed length of Rampart which might include the two Beacon Platforms which have been found in this section. In this position it would be seen from far away and allow the scale of the Wall in the larger landscape to be visualised. Other suitable locations would presumably be in association with one or more of the interpretative facilities where the chance of some supervision would be higher.

AIR PHOTO 3: CROY HILL FROM THE EAST
The line of the Ditch can be clearly seen passing over Croy Hill but beyond
Croy village near to the top of the picture it becomes invisible. The outline
of quarries which are very close to the Wall can be seen near the village.
The outline of Croy Fort can be seen near the small clump of trees in the
centre of the picture. The break in continuity of the Ditch near this same
clump is not due to in-filling; the Ditch was never completed at this point.
The mounds on the right hand side of the picture are industrial waste heaps
now largely overgrown. The Wall is in the guardianship of the Department of
the Environment in this length.

7 priorities, programme and ultimate objectives

The proposals in Chapter 6 represent an attack on the problem on many different fronts and by a variety of means. It is not obvious from reading the list of proposals how the enhancement of the Wall may be expected to proceed from year to year and just what its ultimate degree of protection and presentation to the public will be. A once-and-for-all project to deal with it would be more satisfactory than the little by little approach which is being put forward, but the opportunity for such a comprehensive attack is not there.

Programme of Work

1. The Local Authorities at Bo'ness and Grangemouth will be considering giving more attention to the Wall in their existing parks, and providing interpretation facilities at Kinneil. This could take two to three years to appear on the ground.

2. At Rough Castle a study is required at once of the ultimate Park opportunity, but construction will be long delayed while the mining interests are sorted out, and the park could be ten or more years in coming into being. The interpretation centre which is required there cannot wait so long and must be constructed as an advance project (outside the Guardianship area) together with a better handling of car access and parking. This might realistically be achieved in four years. The planting required at the western end could also be suitably established in advance of the main park, and at the eastern end the walkway connection with Falkirk should continue to be pursued with vigour.

3. The planting in the Cumbernauld extension should proceed as soon as possible, preferably in advance of the prison and industrial construction. The present position concerning land acquisition is not known, but if this is not a difficulty the planting could proceed next year.

4. Between Cumbernauld extension and Croy Hill the motorway is to intervene, and the Wall crosses good farmland. A walking link which would avoid the present detours on the public roads would be highly desirable and an access agreement should be sought here, but its real justification will probably not be there until the population of Cumbernauld extension

builds up and people want to pass on to Croy Hill from Dullatur.

5. The Kirkintilloch/Cumbernauld Park will take many years to construct, but the Wall line is not dependent on its construction for its enhancement but only for the limitation of encroachment, this being an accessible and recreationally valuable stretch already.

6. If the Wester Shirva and Queenzieburn developments are permitted then tree planting should go ahead as a matter of priority.

7. On the section of Wall running into Kirkintilloch the empty Wall reservation should be turned into a well designed public open space with substantial planting to screen the built-up area. Unfortunately this area is not in Designated Countryside.

8. The Balmuildy / Summerston / Crow Hill area requires continuing study to determine whether it will ultimately be a park or not. But like Rough Castle some obvious requirements should not wait for the full park proposal, which is likely to be a ten year affair, but access agreements should be sought to allow the public to walk up Crow Hill from Bearsden, and a small car park should be provided. The Department of the Environment should be asked to state their intention with regard to Balmuildy Fort, and the access agreements and the car park could then be provided in the light of this and the overall design of the park, if any. The complexities in this area make it unlikely that the proposals could be carried out in less than five years.

9. The Braidfield Country Park proposal is barely formulated, but access agreements should not wait for it to come into being. An access should be acquired from the Castlehill end to link with the existing track along the Wall, and a small car park with some interpretative information should be provided. The opportunity could be taken to consider the whole length from M 32.6 to M 34.2 at this time, although part of it is outside the proposed park. This should be possible within two to three years.

10. The rest of the Wall will be enhanced only by the marker masts and wall plaques. This could take five to seven years to implement.

This programme attempts a definition of the best opportunites which exist from the point of view of the qualities of the Wall itself, the degree of difficulty of carrying out any proposal, the apparent public advantage and the likely demand.

There is not one of these four factors which is usefully measurable in terms of this study, and there is some difficulty in knowing how to strike a balance in making the proposals. The intention has been to describe a work load which might be tackled over the next ten years (although the Kirkintilloch/Cumbernauld Park will continue to be implemented long after that date) and to assume that after that time it will have become clearer whether demand is escalating or not.

If the programme is successful in its promotion of the idea of the Wall, it may well be overtaken by its own success and much more may be demanded.

Some Comments on the Demand for Further Access to the Wall

At present demand is very limited. It has to be realised that the Wall has no established place in the cultural history of the country. The more educated know that it exists, but few have searched for it, and of those who have found it the majority have been bitterly disappointed.

The main enthusiasm for the Wall which has been encountered while making the enquiries leading up to this study has come from professional and amateur archaeologists and planning officers; most others have been noticeably ignorant of the Wall and, although polite, uninterested.

The opinion of the Scottish Tourist Board is a fair summary of general reaction. The Wall "does not appear to be of sufficient significance to include in the Board's current promotions even although it is readily accessible from popular existing tourist areas."*

This opinion has to be considered against the astonishing success of the promotion of Bannockburn and Culloden, neither of which have much in the way of authentic remains or authentic environment, but which have flourished due to promotion and invitation to the public to come in. The Wall has much more

Quoted from a letter to the author dated 5th October 1972.

to offer initially than either Bannockburn or Culloden, and appropriate promotion could reverse the opinion of the Tourist Board, while at the same time enhancing the prospects of keeping development away from the Wall and reinforcing the desirable general planning objective of keeping settlements apart by substantial green belts.

The difficulty of foreseeing the future pattern of demand has been not only in relation to the Wall but to recreation space in general. In turning down the Country Park strategy the subjective assessment was made that there would be too much land zoned for Country Parks to be taken up within the next fifteen years.

The Possibility of Reducing the Proposals of Chapter 6

The question then arises whether or not the proposals of Chapter 6 are more than can be justified immediately. Perhaps even where the proposals are agreed to be desirable, they should not all qualify for immediate implementation.

It is not easy to make a list of priorities. This study has been commissioned precisely because there are so many pressures and uncertainties along the Wall line, and it has not so much solved them as parcelled them out as separate problems still requiring further work to reach a solution.

Therefore studies of the future of Rough Castle (2 above) and Summerston (3) are important priorities; the various planting projects are among the more straightforward proposals which should not be delayed (3, 6 and 7), Bo'ness and Grangemouth have existing parks where there is least obstruction to immediate implementation and the masts

and wall markers are the most essential proposal of them all (10).

This leaves only Braidfield Park (9) which has perhaps less recreational justification, Kirkintilloch/Cumbernauld Park, which in spite of plenty of recreational justification may take time to be implemented, and the small matter of access agreements between Dullatur and Croy Hill.

The Possibility of Doing More than the Proposals of Chapter 6

If the climate of opinion swings round to doing much more than the proposals suggest within the next ten to fifteen years, then a different kind of problem begins to arise from those which have so far been considered.

It would be necessary to do two things:

1. Start to take over agricultural land which is thriving, for the sake of the Wall alone, without any expectation of other recreational advantage. This study does not go as far as that.

2. Where the Wall is fragmented by major obstacles the expense of bridging, tunnelling or otherwise circumventing them would have to be faced. This study does not make any recommendations which involve this.

Although additional Country Parks might not be implemented within the period of ten to fifteen years, there could be some advantage in reserving the land for them, although to a large extent this advantage is already achieved through the Amenity Zone idea. It would be foolhardy to speculate on the requirements after ten to fifteen years, as the immediate period holds so many uncertainties, but it is anticipated that the proposals described here will form a balanced basis of action for at least that period, after which a further assessment will require to be made.

8 photographic survey

The complexity of the circumstances of the Wall, the access to it and views from it, is well demonstrated by Figure 2, which also explains the difficulty of trying to give a clear description or a complete photographic coverage.

A partial coverage is given in Plates 9 and 10, which show thirty-six views, eighteen in a westerly direction and eighteen in an easterly direction, each taken standing on the line of the Wall and pointing as nearly as possible along its length. In theory this scheme was intended to give one photograph per mile of the length, but this idea has not been rigorously carried through, as it leads to many interesting points being missed. Instead, some care has been taken to try to get illustrations which show the Wall line in its many differing appearances, while giving as balanced an impression as possible. For this reason the photographs include many sites where no trace of the Wall is to be seen, and ignore others where there may be substantial remains. The selection of the photographs is in the last analysis arbitrary, but it is intended that the descriptions which accompany them will explain and justify their choice.

Many of the photographs are taken at places without names on the Map, and so can only be accurately identified by the mileage along the Wall, which can be read off the Maps. In addition to this mileage figure, the nearest name on the map to the point from which the photograph was taken is given as an aid to location, although it may not be an accurate description.

M 1.7 **Kinneil House**

Here housing shown on the left has been kept back from the Wall line under the existing Development Control procedures. A fine avenue up to Kinneil House, seen on the right, is almost parallel with the Wall line which runs through the buildings; the walled garden beyond encloses the site of the Fort. New tree planting, foreground, pays no regard to the Wall line.

M 3.9 **Inveravon**

The Ditch can be seen climbing the hillside parallel with the Grangemouth Town Council artificial ski-slope, and entering the Golf course beyond the hedge line. This is part of the Polmonthill area where it is recommended that there is scope for improved recognition of, and public access to, the Wall.

M 6.0 **Beancross**

The field in the middle distance is the site of Mumrills Fort which is encroached upon by housing and cut by the public road behind the trees on the right. Plate 10 shows the view from the same place looking east. It is a fine observation point, but one from which no remains of the Wall can be seen.

M 9.1 **Bantaskine**

The Ditch is well preserved but overgrown in a woodland which is a children's playground surrounded by housing. Archaeology might be better served by cutting the trees down, but children's play would be almost eliminated thereby.

M 9.9 **Tamfourhill**

The Ditch is here well preserved in a woodland, but permanently full of water. This is part of the length which should be top priority for Guardianship or acquisition on grounds of linking up Watling Lodge with Rough Castle, but here also the woods are an asset, insulating the Wall from a very close and parallel running public road.

M 10.1 **Tamfourhill**

Well preserved Ditch in semi-natural woodland. The notice draws attention to the problem of having a maintenance policy which will be an "outward expression of Guardianship" which will be sufficient to convince that the land is "in use" as an Ancient Monument and not merely derelict or unused.

M 12.8 **Seabegs Wood**

Well preserved Ditch climbs the hillside away from the public road. The construction of the concrete retaining wall along the roadside when the road was widened, removing some of the outer mound, was opposed by the Department of the Environment both on grounds of removing part of the monument and on aesthetic grounds that the concrete was an unsuitable material.

M 14.75 **Castlecary**

The view is from the Fort, which has a few trees on it at present, looking over the double carriageway of the A 80 towards the industrial complex beyond, through which the Wall passes. The photograph does not show the full width of the road, which forms one of the major discontinuities in the Wall caused by large new roads, and effectively divides the Cumbernauld section from the Falkirk section. The railway seen on the left crossing the bridge bisects the Fort.

M 17.9 **Croy Hill**

The Ditch climbing the hill makes a striking picture, although its actual dimensions are well below full size, due to the short turf and lack of distracting elements in the view.

M 19.8 **Bar Hill**

The Wall line here is visible from afar due to a corridor through the woods having been left unplanted. The trees prevent the enjoyment of the outward views from the Wall line for some distance but the view is clear from the summit and the definition of the line of the Wall by the gap in the trees is a valuable marker.

M 24.6 **Adamslee**

More intensive farming now begins, and there is nothing of the Wall to be seen as it crosses the fields from Kirkintilloch to Glasgow Bridge.

M 26.25 **Cadder**

The canal crosses the Wall hard by Cadder Fort. Its banks are a pleasant ground for strolling and fishing, but there is no evidence of the Wall itself. Cadder Fort has been excavated for sand.

M 27.05 **Wilderness Plantation**

The Ditch can be seen in the foreground, petering out in a flat area of sanitary landfill near Wilderness Plantation. It would not be distinguishable from a chance dip in the land to any unlearned observer.

M 28.2 **Balmuildy**

The Wall line crosses the view in a wide zig-zag in this photograph, crossing the River Kelvin near the left-hand side, climbing Crow Hill in the right-hand middle distance and going off left again towards Castlehill which is seen as skyline trees on the extreme left. Public access should be sought to the top of Crow Hill, which commands views of the Wall line in both directions.

M 29.6 **Crow Hill**

Views towards Bearsden and Castlehill beyond, from Crow Hill. The escarpment has now disappeared and the Wall line travels from small hilltop to small hilltop. The beginning of the Kilpatrick Hills can be seen on the skyline.

M 31.95 **Roman Park, Bearsden**

The iron railing encloses a narrow transect of the Rampart foundation, the Berm and the Ditch. Foundation stones have been disturbed and toppled into the Ditch in spite of the railing. The Park is a narrow band of green along a hilltop, and wholly surrounded by housing.

M 33.7 **Cleddans**

The cart track follows the line of the Wall into the middle distance, after which it swings right towards the golf course and then through the built-up area of Duntocher.

M 36.35 **Mount Pleasant**

View from the edge of the double carriageway road which effectively forms a termination to the length of the Wall which may be visited. From the road onward the railway and the built-up area make fruitless any attempt to follow it to the site of the Roman harbour on the Clyde.

1.7

3.9

6.0

9.1

9.9

10.1

12.8

14.75

17.9

19.8

24.6

26.25

27.05

28.2

29.6

31.95

33.7

36.35

M 36.35 Mount Pleasant

The line of the Wall is straight down the centre of the picture across the arable fields and passing through the narrow gap between the excavation for the Erskine Bridge approach roads and the white building which is a new Gas Governor. The latter clearly impinges on the immediate environs of the Wall, here invisible, and at the moment quite difficult to visit. Restrictions on the placing of this Gas Governor would have resulted from the zonings suggested in this study, taking a very long term view of the necessity to protect the monument from too close encroachment even when no immediate public interest is likely to be shown in the area being encroached upon in the foreseeable future.

M 34.8 Golden Hill

The Wall line passes down the scruffy lane on the left of the picture, crosses the Duntocher Burn, then climbs up the hill to the top where stood Duntocher Fort. Halfway up the hill a tiny railed off rectangle encloses a section of the foundation of the Rampart.

M 32.8 Castlehill

Castlehill is the most conspicuous feature of the Wall in the landscape and it appears distantly in various other photographs on Plate 9. In this picture the Ditch descends the hill with a thick hedgerow growing in the bottom of it which is an aid to seeing it from a distance but a detraction at close quarters. The hedgerow running north and south hides a minor road to Drumchapel which is in a deep cutting. West of the cutting, picture foreground, the Ditch is either invisible or hard to detect.

M 29.6 Crow Hill

Crow Hill affords a long view to the east, the line of the Wall running right to left in the picture past Wilderness Plantation which forms the centre skyline woodland.

M 25.0 Glasgow Bridge

The Wall line crosses the canal close to Glasgow Bridge and then travels over good farming land to Kirkintilloch. Nothing of it is to be seen on the ground at this point.

M 23.2 Kirkintilloch

Housing here is set back allowing the Wall line to remain in open land between it and the canal. There are no visible remains but the opportunity exists of making this into a more meaningfully organised public open space.

M 21.2 Shirva

The Wall line lies in the field just north of the road, so close that walking on the road is virtually walking along the Wall. In this sort of situation a case might be made for a public roadside footpath at the next road improvement.

M 20.5 Twechar

An overgrown hedgerow both marks the line of the Wall and obscures the fact that the Ditch remains to be seen as a shallow depression.

M 17.9 Wester Dullatur

The Ditch here shows a broad depression much flattened out by repeated cultivation. At present detours around the fields on the public roads are necessary to pass from one part of the Wall where there is a right of way to another. A right of way along the Wall line through the agricultural fields may be difficult to negotiate but would be desirable to link up the important Cumbernauld and Croy Hill sections.

M 16.15 Cumbernauld Airstrip

Well defined Ditch with a fine belt of trees, unfortunately on the northern and not the southern side, stops abruptly and changes to a section with little or no trace of the Wall left.

M 11.8 High Bonnybridge

Well defined Ditch crossing a bleak field. Housing development off the picture to the right could be screened out by planting on the south side of the Wall with advantage both to the section seen in the photograph and to the Rough Castle section immediately beyond it.

M 11.2 Rough Castle

Pylons, factory chimneys and the smell of fish-meal detract from Rough Castle, but its moor- and woodland character and the well preserved Wall and Fort still make it a very suitable subject for a Country Park. The photograph shows the Fort immediately beyond the pylons and the Ditch and remains of the Rampart running right to left.

M 9.55 Summerford

Development Control has kept building off the line of the Wall fairly successfully in recent years, but this photograph shows a failure in this respect. The factory is built on top of the Wall as it enters the Guardianship area at Watling Lodge.

M 7.4 Callendar Park

Well defined Ditch near high flats in Callendar Park. The conifers hide northern Falkirk from the Wall. There is no indication that this is a Roman remain and few of the many people who pass it daily are likely to be aware of it.

M 6.0 Beancross

The Wall line runs from the centre bottom of the photograph to the right hand skyline and then along the skyline to the left hand margin. The Motorway and its slip roads effectively break up the continuity of the Wall. There are three such breaks at present, and more are planned.

M 5.0 Polmont

Here the Wall line, nominally visible, traverses a tree nursery and a small coniferous wood. This section is included in the Polmonthill area which should receive further study.

M 2.7 Kinneil Farms

The photograph looks along the Wall line over agricultural fields partly in the ownership of Bo'ness Town Council to the Park beyond and to Bo'ness itself. This section is in the Kinneil area which should receive further study.

M 0.85 Grahamsdyke

The main road follows the Wall line off and on all the way from its eastern end to Falkirk, effectively burying it. Unfortunately, because the road does not follow the Wall consistently, but constantly leaves it, it is an unsatisfactory experience to try to follow the Wall by road; most particularly as it is only when the Wall is not under the road that there is anything to be seen.

36.35

34.8

32.8

29.6

25.0

23.2

21.2

20.5

17.9

16.15

11.8

11.2

9.55

7.4

6.0

5.0

2.7

0.85

APPENDIX 1

1972 STATE OF SCHEDULING AND GUARDIANSHIP

	Scheduled	Guardianship	LA Ownership
Carriden Fort	S		
Harbour Road, Bo'ness	SP 510′		
Kinneil—Nether Kinneil	S 4 000′		
Nether Kinneil—Inveravon	S 6 200′		
Inveravon—River Avon incl. Fort	S 1 000′		
Polmont Hill	S 2 550′		Grangemouth
Little Kerse	S 1 650′		
Mumrills incl. Fort	S 2 600′		
Callendar Park	S 4 850′		Falkirk
Bantaskine	S 1 200′		
Watling Lodge : NS 866798-863798		G 1 100′	
Watling Lodge—Rough Castle	S 5 500′		
Rough Castle incl. Fort : NS 845800-835798			
Bonnyside House, Elf Hill	S 1 800′		
Roman Road, Seabegs	380′		
Seabegs Place—Seabegs Wood	S 1 500′		
Seabegs Wood : NS 815794-811792		G 1 400′	
Seabegs—Castlecary	S 6 000′		
Castlecary incl. Fort : NS 791784-778781		G 1 100′	
Garnhall : NS 784781-778779		G 1 450′	
Tollpark : NS 778779-769777		G 3 100′	Cumbernauld
Arniebog	S 1 800′		Cumbernauld
Westerwood incl. Fort	S 2 500′		
Westerwood—Dullatur Colliery : NS 756773-751772		G 1 600′	
East Dullatur	S 1 200′		
Wester Dullatur	S 600′		
Croy Hill incl. Fort : NS 738769-725762		G 5 500′	
Croy—Girnal Hill	SP 2 300′		
Girnal Hill—Barhill Cottage	S 1 500′		
Bar Hill incl. Fort : NS 713762-706759		G 2 400′	
Bar Hill—Twechar	S 1 900′		
Twechar	SP 1 580′		
Shirva—Auchendavy incl. Fort :	S 7 100′		
Whitehill	S 400′		
Hillhead—Kirkintilloch	SP 2 100′		
Kirkintilloch Fort	S 450′		Kirkintilloch
Adamslee—Glasgow Bridge incl. Fortlet	S 3 000′		
Glasgow Bridge—Cadder	S 6 000′		
Cadder—Cawder	SP 2 400′		
Cawder	S 2 100′		
Wilderness Plantation	S 2 500′		
Balmuildy incl. Fort	S 3 500′		
Balmuildy—New Kilpatrick Cemetery	S 9 300′		
New Kilpatrick	S 900′		
Bearsden, Thorn Road	S 1 000′		Bearsden
Castle Hill incl. Fort	S 2 900′		
Hutcheson Hill	S 1 400′		1 200′ Glasgow
Cleddans	S 4 800′		
Golden Hill, Duntocher, incl. Fort	S 1 050′		Dunbartonshire
Beeches Road—Old Kilpatrick	S 7 300′		

S — Scheduled   105 530′ — 20.3 miles

SP — Scheduling proceeding   8 890′ — 1.7 miles

G — Guardianship   20 850′ — 4 miles

TEMPORARY CAMPS SCHEDULED

1. Muirhouses
2. Kinglass
3. Inveravon (3)
4. Polmont Hill
5. Little Kerse
6. Wester Carmuirs
7. Milnquarter
8. Dalnair
9. Garnhall
10. Adamslee
11. Buchley

APPENDIX 2

THE PROPOSED DEFINITION OF "SIGNIFICANT DEVELOPMENT" IN THE AMENITY ZONES

The proposal is that Significant Development should be referred to the Scottish Development Department by the Local Planning Authorities within the Amenity Zones for informal discussion.

Significant Development has yet to be defined, but the suggestion being put forward by the Scottish Development Department is that it should include the following:

1. All mineral workings.

2. All industrial development except small additions to existing buildings.

3. Large "service" developments such as warehousing, road haulage depots, local authority depots etc.

4. Tourist and recreation development involving substantial new building (hotels etc.) or visually important items such as caravan sites.

5. Large institutional or community buildings.

6. All residential development except alterations to existing property, and except single dwellings where the Local Planning Authority is satisfied that the development will be unobtrusive and will not be a precedent for numerous other permissions.

7. Any other development which the Local Planning Authority considers will significantly alter the degree of Countryside character that the area possesses.

APPENDIX 3

ACKNOWLEDGEMENTS

In the preparation of this report, information and help has been sought from the following bodies. The time and trouble which they have taken is here gratefully acknowledged.

Maps 1, 2 and 3 are based on the Ordnance Survey map with the sanction of the Controller of H.M. Stationery Office, and Crown Copyright is reserved. The aerial photographs are reproduced by permission of Dr. J. K. St. Joseph, and copyright is reserved.

Scottish Development Department
Department of the Environment
Cumbernauld Development Corporation
Dunbarton County Council
Lanark County Council
Stirling County Council
West Lothian County Council
Bearsden Burgh Council
Bishopbriggs Burgh Council
Bo'ness Burgh Council
Clydebank Burgh Council
Falkirk Burgh Council
Grangemouth Burgh Council
Kirkintilloch Burgh Council
Glasgow Corporation
British Waterways Board
Lanarkshire Water Board
Lower Clyde Water Board
South of Scotland Electricity Board
The Nature Conservancy

Department of Agriculture and Fisheries for Scotland
Forestry Commission
Scottish Tourist Board
Scottish Landowners Federation
National Farmers Union of Scotland
Scottish Woodland Owners Association
National Trust for Scotland
Scottish Civic Trust
Association for the Protection of Rural Scotland
Scottish Rights of Way Society
Saltire Society
Scottish Inland Waterways Association
Council of British Archaeology
Glasgow Archaeological Society
Hunterian Museum, Glasgow
National Museum of Antiquities, Edinburgh
Institute of Geological Sciences
National Playing Fields Association
Ramblers Association
Scottish Countryside Activities Council
Scottish Sports Council
Scottish Wildlife Trust

Much of the work in the preparation of this study was done by Colin McKerchar, assisted by Ian McGowan and Anne Watson. My thanks are also due to staff of the Countryside Commission for Scotland for preparing the manuscript for publication and designing its presentation.

BIBLIOGRAPHY

BALLANTYNE, J. and HARPER, R. J. *The Forth-Clyde Canal — A Preliminary Report*

MATTHEW, R. A. and JOHNSON-MARSHALL, P. *Grangemouth/Falkirk — Regional Survey and Plan.* Vol. 2 Physical Planning Aspects. Edinburgh University.

DUFFIELD, B. S. and OWEN, M. L. *Leisure + Countryside a Study of Recreation in Lanarkshire.* Edinburgh University Department of Geography.

EVANS, F. J., O.B.E. *A Study for a Footways System North of Glasgow.*

McLELLAN, A. G., B.Sc., Ph.D. *The Distribution of Sand and Gravel Deposits in West Central Scotland.*

ROBERTSON, Dr. Anne. *The Antonine Wall*, Glasgow Archaeological Society 1960.

TRAVIS, Prof. A. S. (Director of Study): *Recreation Planning for the Clyde.* Scottish Tourist Board 1970.

Special Reports:

1. Stirling County Council's Report on the Antonine Wall.

2. Stirling County Council's Survey Report on Forth and Clyde Canal

3. Stirling County Council's Report on Banton Loch Country Park.

4. Bishopbriggs Canal Study for the Burgh of Bishopbriggs, prepared by Wm. Gillespie & Associates, Nov. 1971.

5. Cumbernauld Draft Report on the Area between Kirkintilloch, Cumbernauld and Kilsyth.

6. Bearsden Burgh Guide.

Planning Authorities: Development Plans.